BLUEPRINT
Geography Key Stage 2 Copymasters

Second edition

Stephen Scoffham

Colin Bridge

Terry Jewson

Stanley Thornes (Publishers) Ltd

First published in 1992 by:
Stanley Thornes (Publishers) Ltd
Ellenborough House
Wellington Street
CHELTENHAM GL50 1YW
England

Reprinted 1993 (twice), 1994 (twice)

Second edition 1995

Reprinted 1995

A catalogue record for this book is available from the British Library.

ISBN 0–7487–2217–3

Typeset by Tech-Set, Gateshead, Tyne & Wear
Printed and bound in Great Britain.

CONTENTS AND SKILLS LIST

COPYMASTER	DESCRIPTION	LINKS TO THE PROGRAMME OF STUDY
21. Signs and symbols	The children make drawings of signs and symbols in the immediate environment.	Use symbols and keys
22. Adventure playground	A game in which children select items for their own adventure playground using a dice.	
23. Classroom measurements	Working from a scale plan of a classroom, the children calculate distances between named places.	Measure direction and distance
24. Direction finder	The children make a tracing of the direction finder to use on a map of their area.	
25. Barriers	The children colour a map of south-west England and discover the main physical barriers.	
26. Scale bar	An exercise in which children calculate the distance from London to other cities with a scale bar.	
27. School trail	The children record what they can see, hear, touch and do at different points around the school.	Follow routes
28. Different directions	The children make a list of countries in different compass directions from the UK. Atlases needed.	Use atlas index and contents
29. Rivers and mountains	Working from an atlas index, the children find out about famous rivers and mountains.	
30. Country profile	The children draw a sketch map and complete a datafile about a country of their choice.	
31. Comparisons	The children compare their own area with another part of the UK. Atlases needed.	
32. Continent cube	Using crayons, glue and scissors, the children construct continent cubes. Best duplicated on card.	
33. UK mountains and rivers	The children colour a key and name some major UK landscape features. Atlases needed.	Maps A, B and C
34. UK countries and capitals	The children identify the different countries and capital cities in the UK.	
35. UK jigsaw	The children cut out the countries of the UK and construct a map. Scissors and glue needed.	
36. Railway routes	Using a map of the UK, the children draw railway routes and list physical obstacles. Atlases needed.	
37. Motorway routes	Using a map of England and Wales, the children discover the places most accessible by motorway.	
38. European capitals	The children identify European capitals on a map and measure their distance from London.	
39. European countries	Working from outline shapes, the children name ten European countries. Atlases needed.	
40. World mountains rivers and deserts	The children annotate a map of world landscape features.	
41. World countries	The children colour selected countries on the world map using colours listed in a key.	
42. Places worldwide	An informal assessment sheet using the places marked on map C.	
43. School address	The children write the different components of their address on a diagram.	Studying the local area
44. Weather profile	The children join points on a profile to record the weather in their area.	

COPYMASTER	DESCRIPTION	LINKS TO THE PROGRAMME OF STUDY
45. Wet and dry	A study of a sample school which illustrates how different surfaces retain water.	Studying the local area
46. Street furniture	An exercise in which the children identify missing items of street furniture and suitable local sites.	
47. New schemes	Working from a prepared list, the children decide which new schemes would be suitable for their area.	
48. Impact studies	The children consider the advantages and disadvantages of the projects planned for their area.	
49. Plan a village	The children design a village of their own by drawing symbols on a map.	
50. Different places	The children compare a rural and urban locality using pictures.	Studying a contrasting UK locality
51. Best place	A simple survey in which children decide on the environment in which they would most like to live.	
52. Connections	The children analyse the places around the local area and a contrasting locality. Maps needed.	
53. Questions	A checklist of questions to help children study a distant place.	Studying an overseas locality
54. Differences in wealth	Using average incomes, the children discover differences in wealth around the world.	
55. River systems	The children write sentences to go with pictures of the different parts of a river system.	Parts of a river system
56. Water symbols	An exercise to help children identify water symbols. Ordnance Survey maps needed.	
57. Rivers worldwide	The children learn about major rivers of the world by researching information from an atlas.	
58. Wear and tear	The children find out about different examples of wear and tear around their school.	River erosion
59. Local landscapes	The children list names for different local landscape features.	
60. World landscapes	An exercise in which the children name landscape features around the world. Atlases needed.	
61. Deltas	The children identify and name major river deltas around the world.	
62. Weather conditions	The children devise drawings to illustrate different temperature, wind and cloud conditions.	Local weather conditions
63. Sun and shade	A comparison of sun and shade temperatures in the school grounds. Electric thermometers needed.	
64. Different sites	A survey of different sites around the school providing information for a computer datafile.	
65. Site conditions	A study of site conditions around the school showing how they can be grouped together.	
66. London climate graph	Working from statistics in a table, the children plot a temperature and rainfall graph for London.	Seasonal weather patterns
67. The farmer's year	The children complete a seasonal activity dial for a farm they have visited or studied.	
68. Summer and winter	The children colour and explain two diagrams showing the Earth in June and December.	

	DESCRIPTION	LINKS TO THE PROGRAMME OF STUDY
69. Weather worldwide	The children complete a world map of polar, desert and rainforest areas.	Weather worldwide
70. Contrasts	Three different drawings show how temperature and rainfall combine to affect vegetation.	
71. Rainforest products	The children identify and label different rainforest products.	
72. House plants	An exercise relating equatorial, desert and polar plants to the home environment.	
73. Types of town	The children colour and label drawings of the key features of different towns.	Types of settlement
74. Historic towns	The children make a list of Roman town names. Historic map needed.	
75. City search	A word search puzzle in which children find the hidden names of different UK cities.	
76. Great cities	The children label major cities on a world map. Atlases needed.	
77. Classroom areas	The children identify different areas on a classroom map.	Uses of land
78. School site	Working from a school plan, the children identify different types of land use.	
79. Transport survey	A survey sheet to help analyse traffic in local streets.	
80. Ports and airports	Working from a map of the UK, the children make a list of major ports and airports.	
81. Zones	The children create land use symbols for use on a wall map. Scissors needed.	
82. Factory study	The children can complete this survey sheet either during a site visit or in the classroom.	
83. Changes	The children consider how new facilities and developments affect the local environment.	Land use conflicts
84. Suitable sites	Working from a map, the children select sites which would be suitable for different activities.	
85. New facilities	A questionnaire in which children discover what new facilities people want in the local area.	
86. New motorway	Role play cards illustrating different viewpoints about a new motorway scheme.	
87. Severn barrage	A plan and list of key facts about the proposed Severn barrage.	
88. Channel tunnel	Arguments for and against the Channel tunnel for use in simulation.	
89. Narmada Dams, India	Background information and map of the Narmada River dams. Use to support work on Indian localities.	
90. Carajas Project, Brazil	Details of the Carajas Project. Could be used as part of a project on the rainforest.	
91. Street survey	The children explore opinions about the local environment using word pairs.	Human impact on the environment
92. Pollution problems	The children list local pollution problems and decide how long they will last.	

	DESCRIPTION	LINKS TO THE PROGRAMME OF STUDY
93. Derelict land	Working from a drawing, the children discover some of the problems affecting the landscape.	Human impact on the environment
94. Quarry schemes	The children consider some of the different ways an old quarry could be used.	
95. Water supplies	The children arrange six small drawings to construct a flow diagram. Scissors needed.	
96. Worth preserving?	Using a number scoring system, the children identify the parts of the school to preserve.	Protecting the environment
97. School improvements	The children complete file cards on four possible projects and decide how to implement them.	
98. Improvements trail	The children consider how local problems might be solved.	
99. Special sites	The children devise symbols for special sites and make a list of local examples.	
100. Different landscapes	The children compare features of different landscapes to assess their environmental quality.	
101. National parks	Using a map of Britain, the children label the national parks.	
102. Record sheet		
103. Pupil profile		

INTRODUCTION

These copymasters are intended for children in junior schools working on geography at Key Stage 2. They are linked directly to the activities in the *Teacher's Resource Book*. There are 101 copymasters covering all aspects of the geography curriculum.

The copymasters have been designed to:

- structure practical investigation in the local environment
- reinforce mapwork skills
- introduce a range of recording techniques
- extend the pupil's geographical experience and understanding
- promote discussion, reflection and analysis.
- provide a basis for assessment

The book is structured to follow the sequence of the National Curriculum (1995). It begins with copymasters that develop geographical skills; this is followed by work on places, and finally geographical themes. Two summary sheets are provided at the back for record-keeping purposes. Notes and guidance on how to use the copymasters are given in the *Teacher's Resource Book*.

The copymasters may be used for individual work, group activities or exercises involving the whole class. They are easy to integrate with theme or topic work, and the completed sheets can be added to work files to act as records of achievement. By using the copymasters on a regular basis, you can address the requirements of the geography National Curriculum in an enjoyable and worthwhile way.

Name ______________________________

Geography dictionary

1. Write down the meaning of each of the words below.
2. Working from this list, make up a dictionary with words and pictures.

Letter	Word	Meaning
a	airport	
b	bridge	
c	cliff	
d	desert	
e	environment	
f	factory	
g	garage	
h	house	
i	island	
j	job	
k	kerb	
l	lake	
m	marsh	
n	nature reserve	
o	office	
p	park	
q	quarry	
r	region	
s	slope	
t	town	
u	United Kingdom	
v	valley	
w	waterfall	

Name ____________________

Word picture

Look at each group of words in turn. Colour the circles next to the words which describe your area.

Landscape		Buildings		Transport	
cliff	○	church	○	aeroplane	○
coast	○	factory	○	bike	○
flat	○	garage	○	bus	○
hill	○	hospital	○	car	○
lake	○	hotel	○	ferry	○
marsh	○	house	○	lorry	○
mountain	○	inn	○	motorbike	○
river	○	office	○	ship	○
slope	○	school	○	train	○
valley	○	shop	○	underground	○

Land use		Employment		Environment	
car park	○	bus driver	○	attractive	○
farm	○	butcher	○	clean	○
gardens	○	dentist	○	dirty	○
housing	○	doctor	○	dull	○
industry	○	greengrocer	○	interesting	○
park	○	librarian	○	noisy	○
playground	○	postman	○	quiet	○
road	○	secretary	○	smelly	○
wasteland	○	shopkeeper	○	ugly	○
wood	○	teacher	○	untidy	○

Name ______________________________

Neighbourhood walk

Use this sheet on a walk round your neighbourhood. First write down the name of each stop, then describe what it is like by ticking the boxes.

	Stop ①	Stop ②	Stop ③	Stop ④	Stop ⑤
Landscape					
coast					
flat					
hilly					
streams or rivers					
woods or trees					
Buildings					
church					
factory					
houses					
offices					
shops					
Transport					
car					
cyclist					
lorry					
pedestrian (walker)					
train					
Land use					
farmland					
factories					
housing					
open space					
shops and offices					

Name ________________________________

Direction dial

1. Colour and cut out the circle and arrow.
2. Fix the arrow to the centre of the dial with a fastener.
3. Stand with the dial pointing the way you are looking.
4. Find the angle of different things around you.

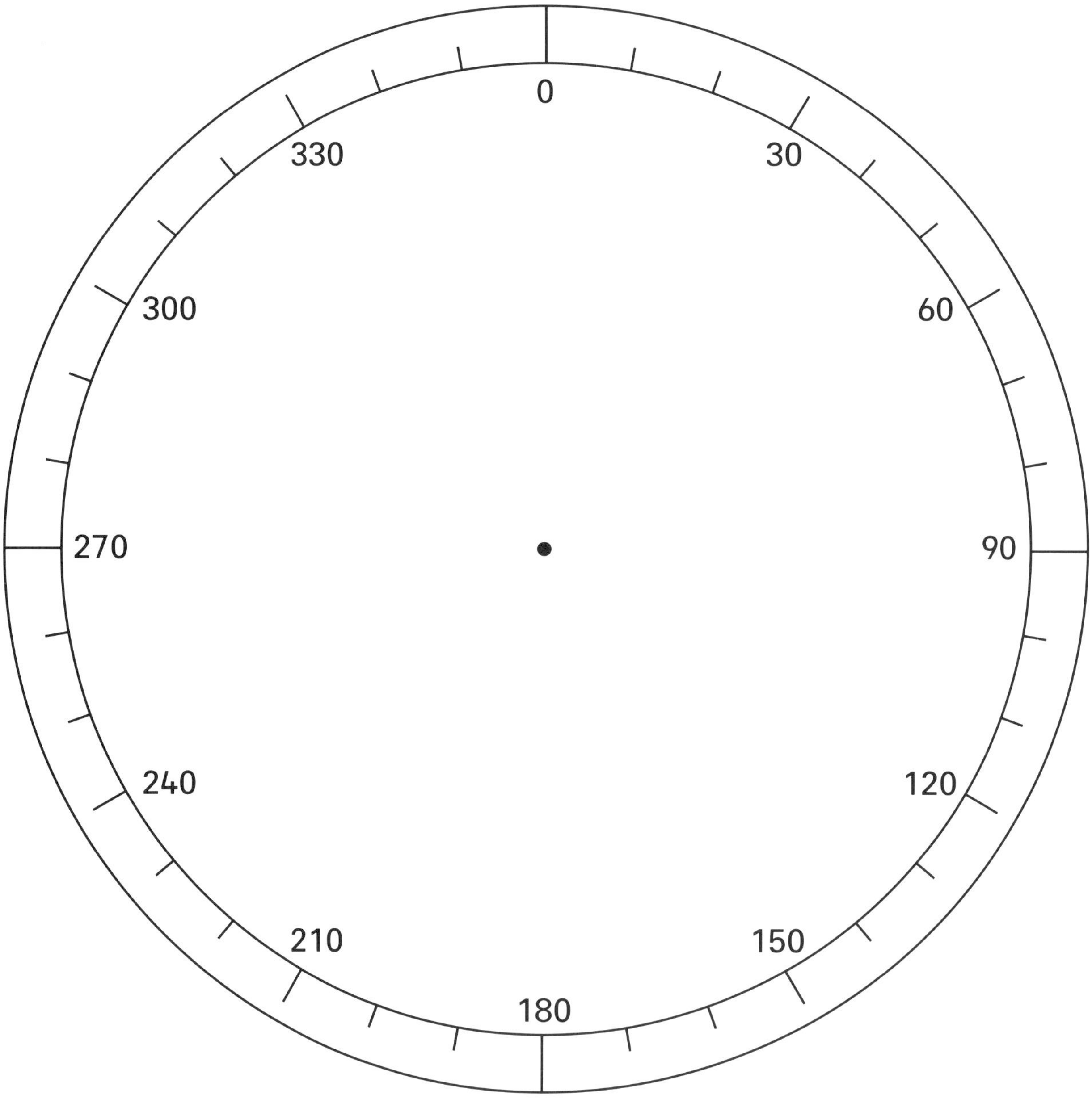

Name ______________________________

School temperatures

1. Measure the temperature in your school or playground at 9.00 a.m., 11.00 a.m., 1.00 p.m. and 3.00 p.m.
2. Write the temperature in the 'bowl' of each thermometer and colour the column to the correct height.

9.00 a.m. **11.00 a.m.** **1.00 p.m.** **3.00 p.m.**

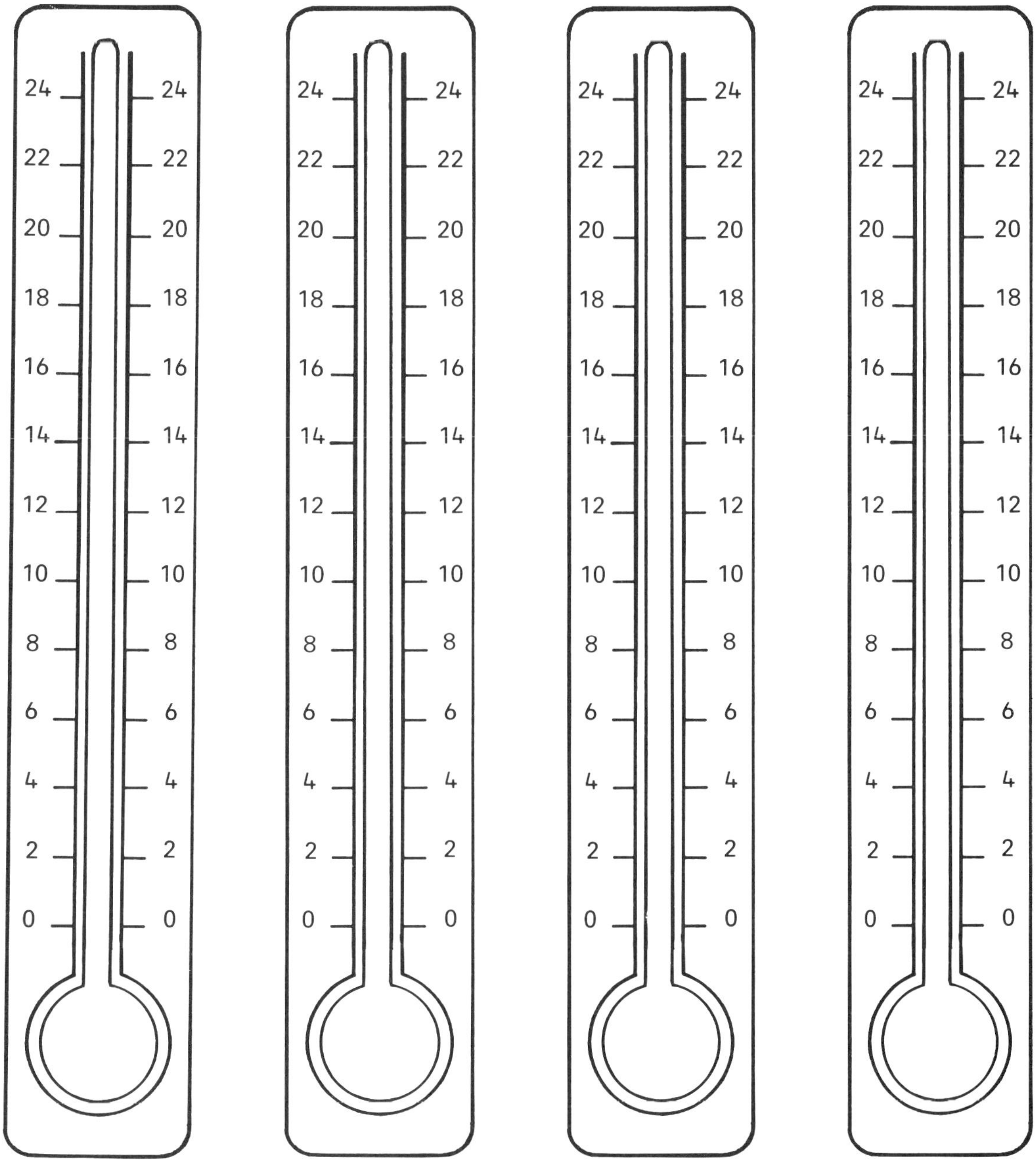

3. Add up the readings and divide by four to find the average for the day.

☐ ÷ 4 ☐

Total **Average**

Name ______________________________

Wind rose

1. Colour a square on the wind rose each day to show the direction of the wind in your area.

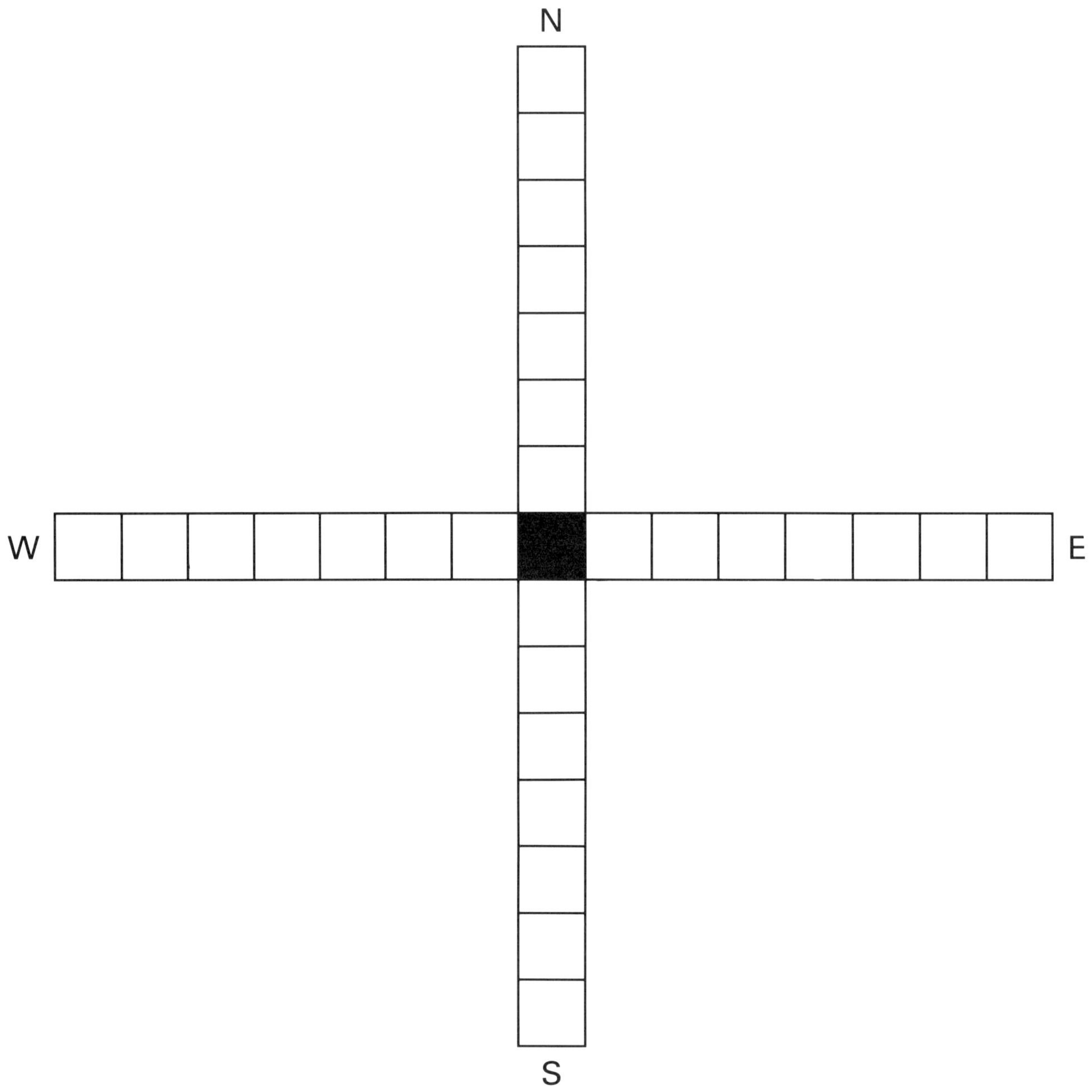

Name ______________________________

Jobs in school

1. Complete the fact files about different jobs in your school.

TEACHER

Name ______________________________

Begins work __________ Finishes work __________

Main tasks ______________________________

____

CARETAKER

Name ______________________________

Begins work __________ Finishes work __________

Main tasks ______________________________

____

SECRETARY

Name ______________________________

Begins work __________ Finishes work __________

Main tasks ______________________________

____

Name ________________________

Postcards

1. Choose two different postcards. Make a simple drawing of each one in the spaces below and name the place that it shows.

Card 1	Card 2

2. Answer each question with a tick or a cross.

Questions	Card1	Card 2
Does it show weather conditions?		
Does it show landscape features (mountains, cliffs, valleys)?		
Does it show houses and buildings?		
Does it show roads, paths or railways?		
Does it show how people travel (cars or buses)?		
Does it show how farmers use the land?		
Does it show places where people work?		
Does it show any pollution problems?		
Does it show how people are caring for the environment?		

3. Which card gives you the most information?

____

4. Write a description of this place on a separate piece of paper.

Name ______________________________

Newspaper articles

1. Read the articles about different parts of the world in a national newspaper.

2. Decide what each article is about by ticking the boxes in the table below.

	Mainland Europe	North and South America	Africa and Asia	Other
Weather				
Wars				
Politics				
Economic Activity				
Health				
Environment				
Sport				
Travel				
Other				

3. Which parts of the world are mentioned most often? ....
   What issues are mentioned most often? ....

Name ______________________________

Using photographs

1. Glue a photograph or postcard in the empty space.

2. Tick the boxes which match the photograph best.

Weather Hot ☐ Cold ☐ Sunny ☐ Cloudy ☐ Snowy ☐

Landscape Seaside ☐ Mountains ☐ Forest ☐ Town ☐

Season Summer ☐ Winter ☐

Place UK ☐ Europe ☐ Far Away ☐

3. Write down two questions you cannot answer from the photograph.

(a) ....

(b) ....

Name ____________________

Weather data

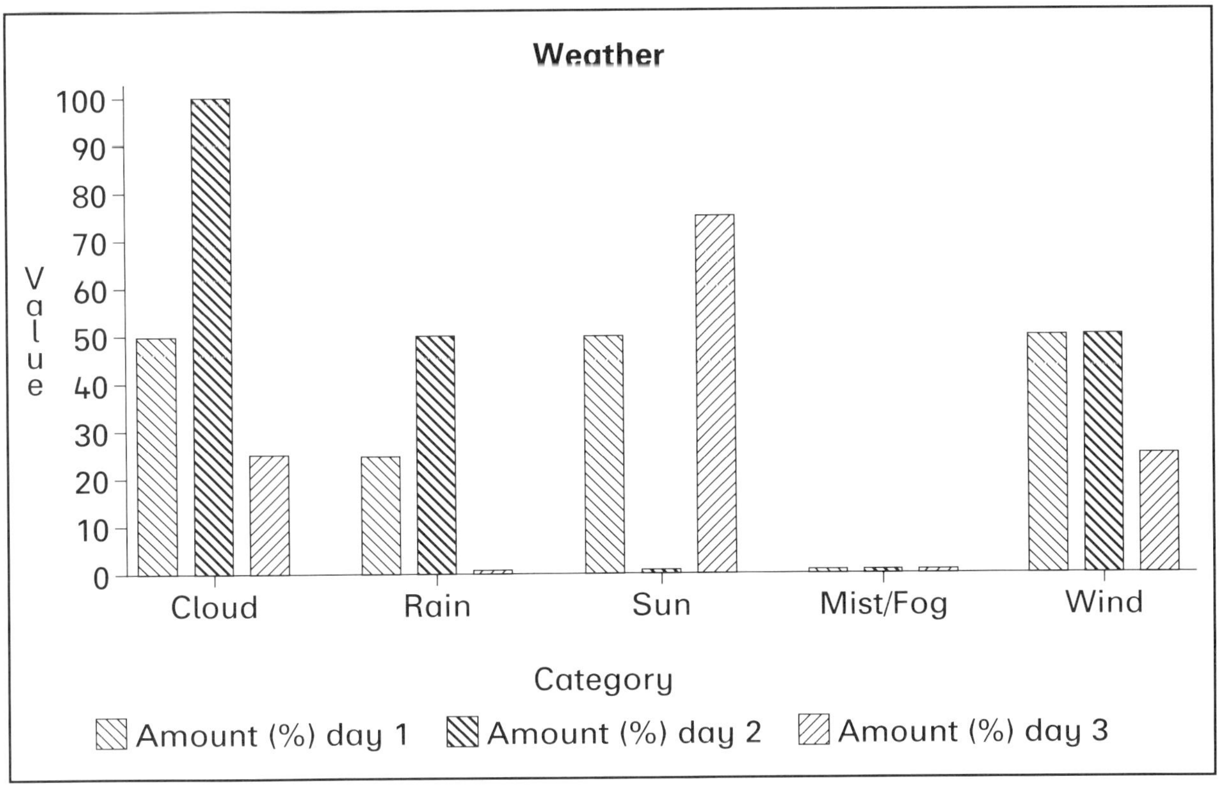

1. Answer the questions using the bar charts of weather data.
   (a) Which day was cloudiest? ....
   (b) Which day was wettest? ....
   (c) Which day was sunniest? ....
   (d) Which two days had the same amount of wind? ....
   (e) When was there 50% sunshine? ....

2. Write a short report about the weather on day 1 ....

....

....

....

Name ______________________________

Plan views

1. Draw a picture of something from your home or classroom in the space opposite. Show the oblique view (top, front and side).

2. Now draw the side and plan views of the same thing in the spaces below.

Oblique view (top, front, side)

Overhead view (plan)

Side view (elevation)

Name ____________________

Aerial photographs

Look carefully at three different aerial photographs. Put a tick or a cross on the chart next to the things you can see in each one.

Landscape features	Photo 1	Photo 2	Photo 3
river			
woods			
fields			
lakes			
sea			
mountains			
cliff			
Human activity	**Photo 1**	**Photo 2**	**Photo 3**
houses			
gardens			
church			
farm			
car park			
shop/supermarket			
factory			
quarry			
railway			
road			
motorway			
bridge			

Name ______________________________

Landmarks

1. Draw pictures of four things which you pass on your journey from home to school.

2. Name the things you have drawn.

3. Show these things on a map of your journey from home to school.

Name ______________________________

Bus routes

1. Look at the table of bus routes from Liverpool.

2. Draw a line on the diagram at the bottom of the page, to show the places where each bus goes.

3. Write the number of each bus route next to the lines.

Bus Number	Route			
33	Liverpool	Widnes	Warrington	Wigan
12	Liverpool	Birkenhead	Ellesmere Port	Warrington
6	Liverpool	Formby	Southport	
8	Liverpool	St Helens	Wigan	Warrington

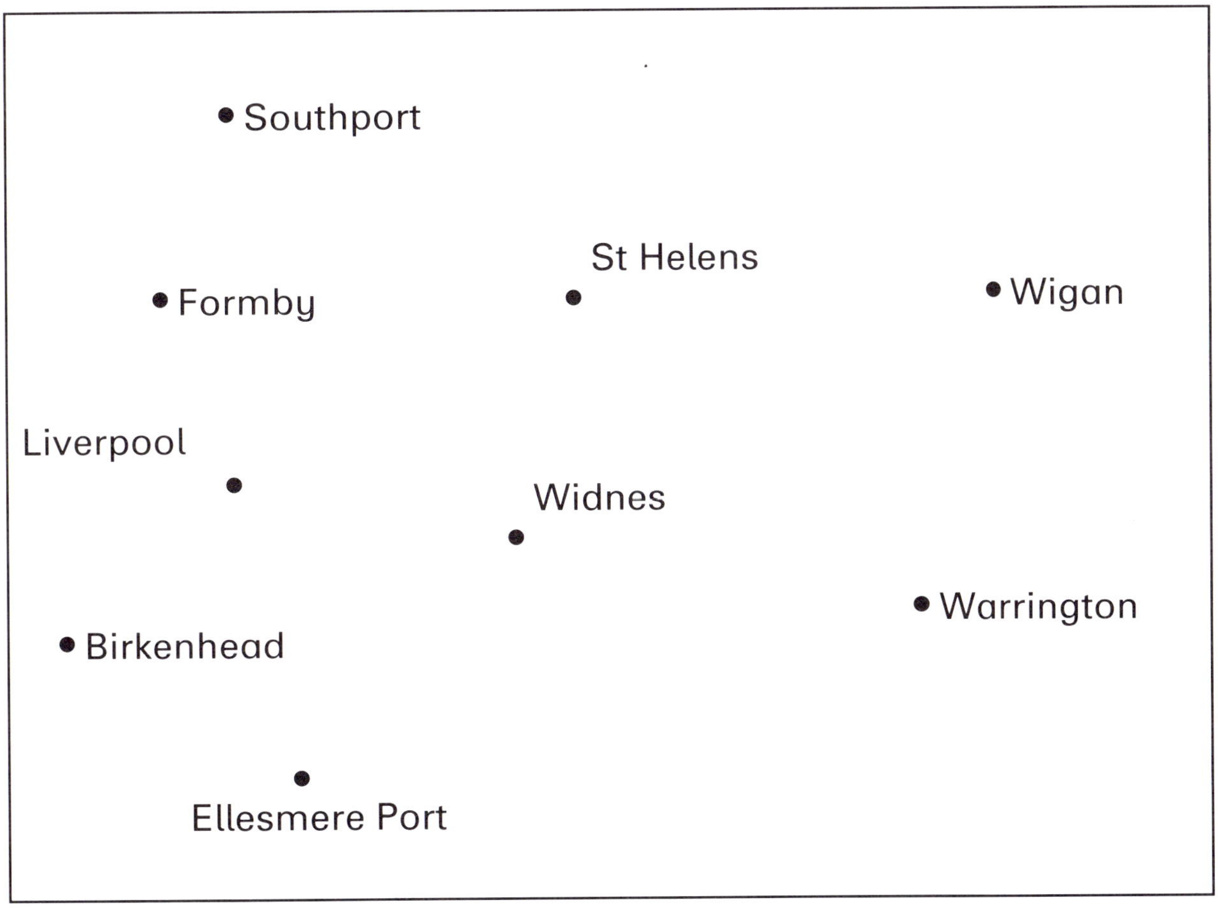

Name ______________________________

Grid board

Draw the things listed below in the correct squares on the board.

pencil A 2   scissors B 3

book B 1   rubber A 1

ruler C 3   compass C 1

3			
2			
1			
	A	B	C

Name ______________________________

Grid picture

1. Write the number of each square in the grid below.
2. Now colour the squares using the colours in the table.

Red	Yellow		Blue	
61, 37	60, 36	62, 34	60, 38	63, 38
61, 35	61, 36	63, 36	60, 37	63, 34
62, 36	62, 38	64, 36	60, 35	64, 38
63, 37	62, 37		60, 34	64, 37
63, 35	62, 35		61, 38	64, 35
			61, 34	64, 34

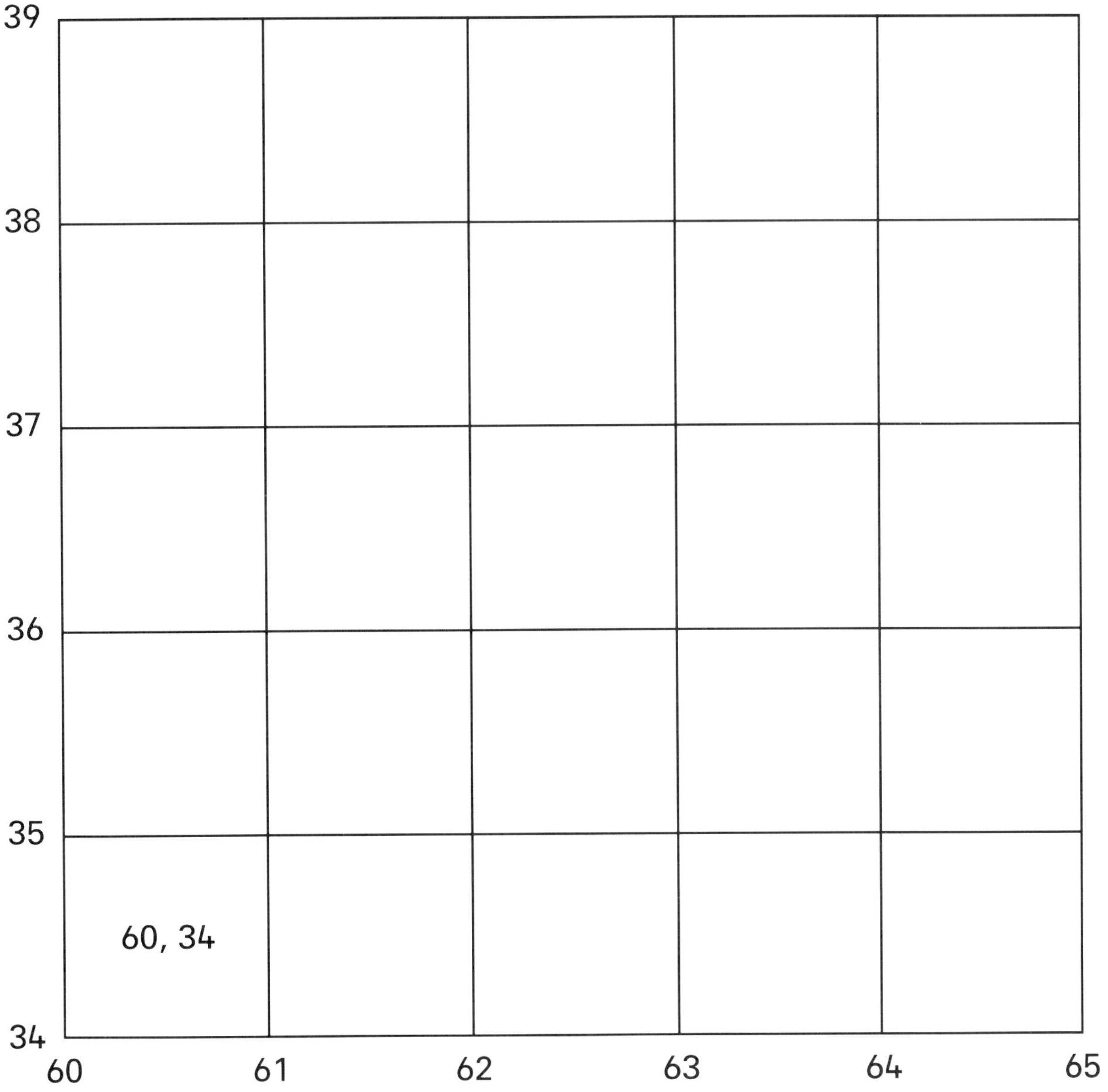

Name ______________________________

Town map

1. Create a grid on the map below by joining the opposite pairs of dots.

2. Give the grid references for the places listed below.

pond ______ petrol station ______ old tree ______

church ______ Post Office ______ flats ______

3. Name one of the things you can find on the following grid squares.

43, 04 ________ 48, 02 ________

46, 06 ________ 49, 01 ________

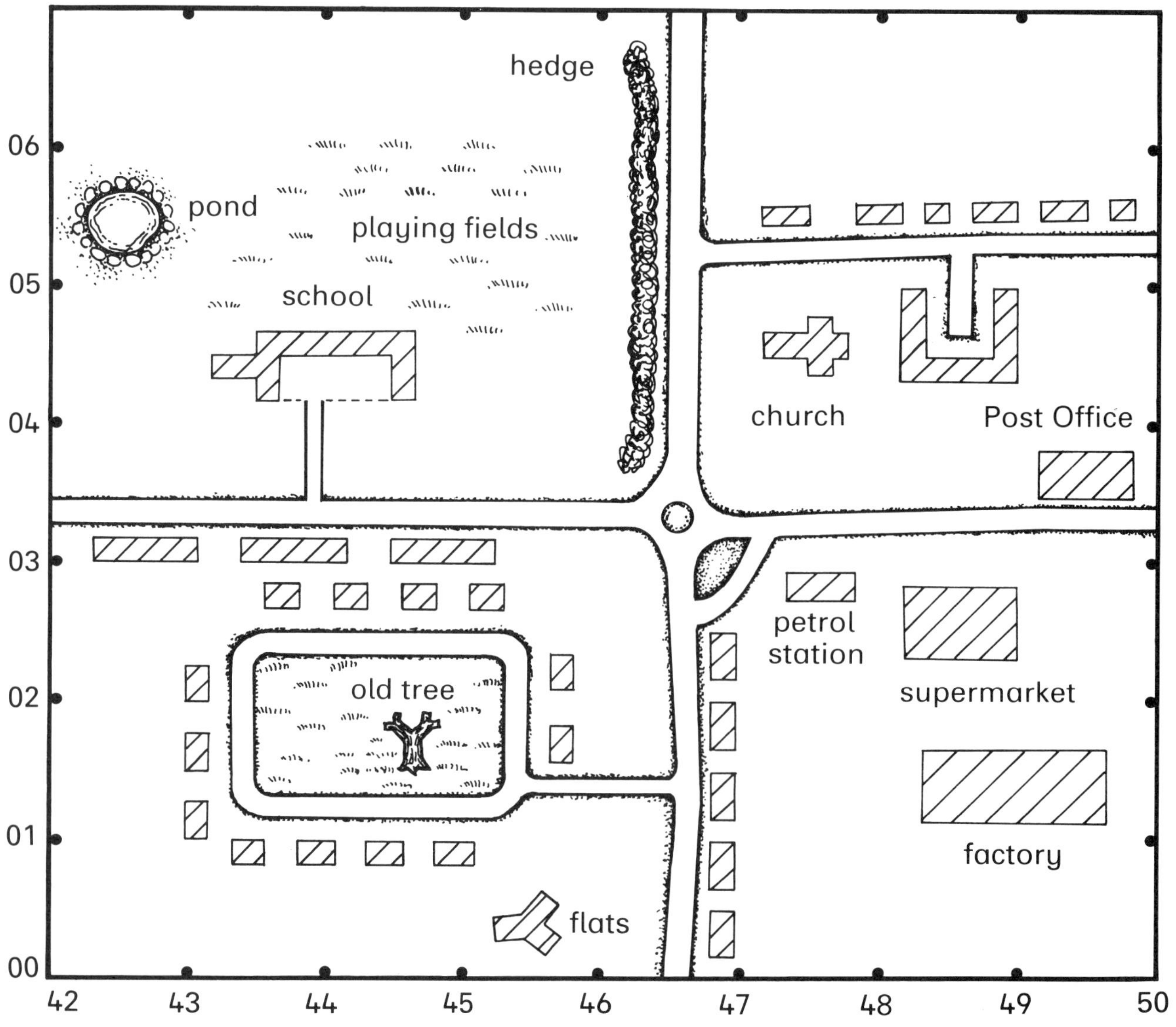

Name ________________________________

Treasure island

1. Cut out the grid squares on the map below. They are all muddled up.

2. Rearrange them in the correct order, and glue them down on a separate sheet of paper.

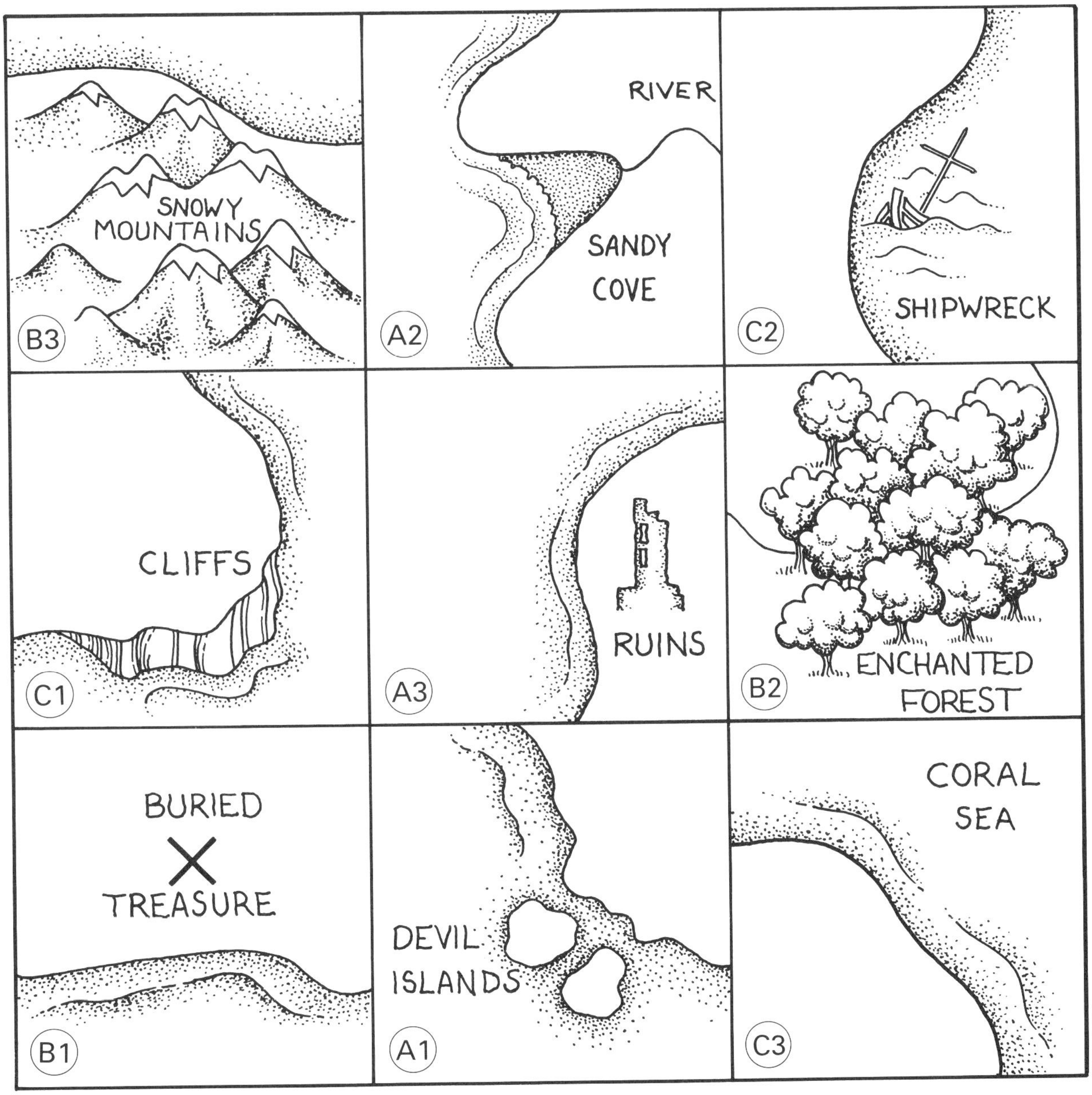

Name ______________________________

Grid squares

1. Colour the map below. Use red for London, green for the countryside and blue for the sea.
2. Join the dots around the edge of the map to make a grid.

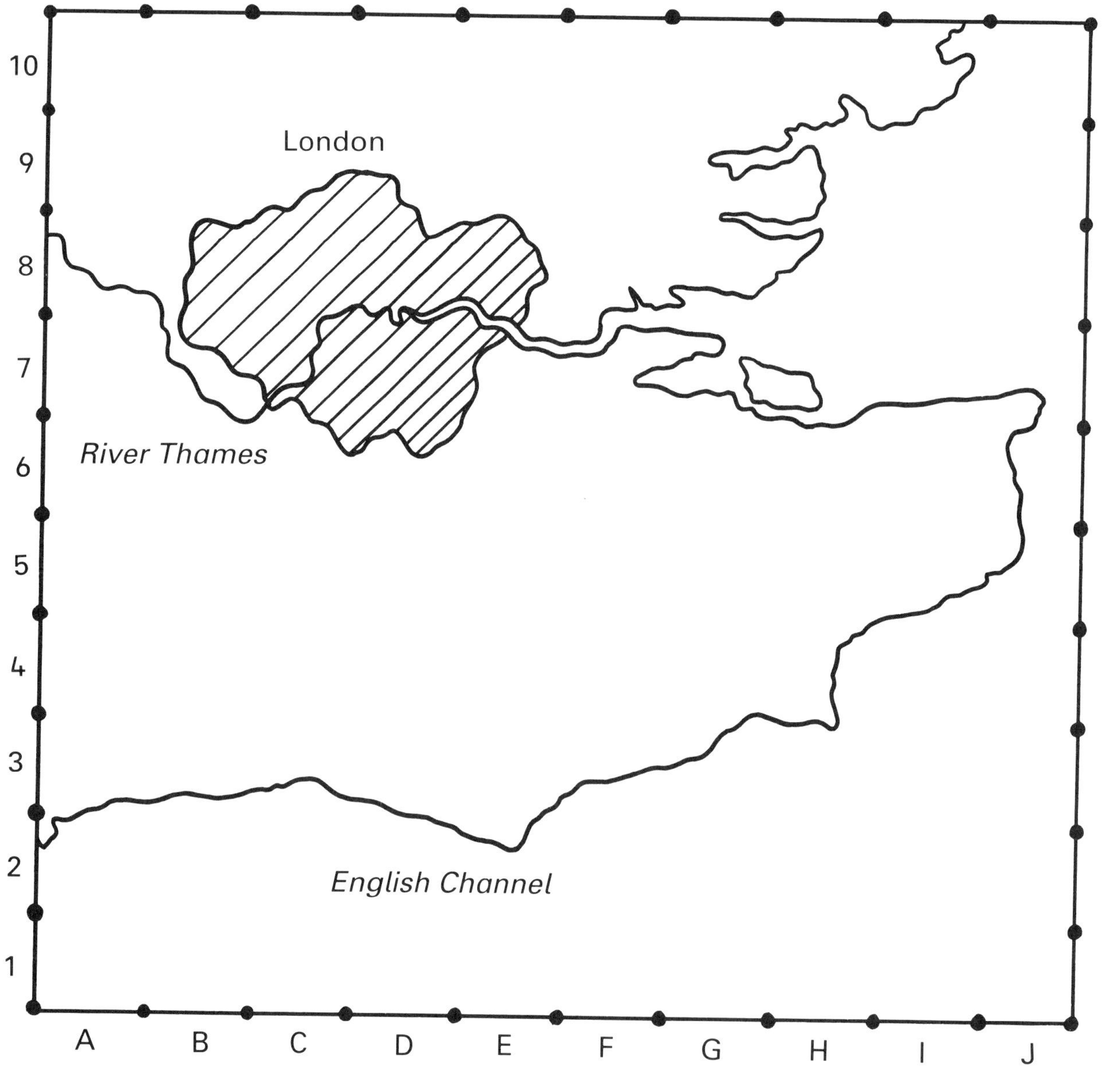

3. Decide if each square is mainly built up, mainly countryside or mainly sea. Start with square A1 and put tally marks in the table below.

	Tally marks	**Total**
mainly built up		
mainly countryside		
mainly sea		

Name ______________________________

Signs and symbols

1. Do drawings of three different signs and symbols you can see in your school or classroom. Say what they mean underneath.

______________	______________	______________
______________	______________	______________
______________	______________	______________

2. Design symbols for each of the places below.

An airport	A National Park	Historic building

Name ______________________________

Adventure playground

1. The items for your adventure playground should be selected at random by throwing a pair of dice. You have twelve goes in all. Each time you throw the dice, add up the total and tick the correct item in the key below.

2. Choose the best place in the playground for the things you have ticked and draw the correct symbols on the plan.

Key

	✓	Item	Symbol
2		pond	
3		pull rings	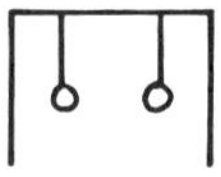
4		logs	
5		see-saw	
6		roundabout	
7		monkey bars	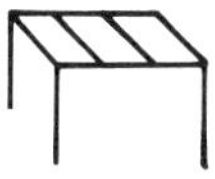
8		stepping stones	
9		slide	
10		balance bars	
11		ladder	
12		nature corner	

Plan

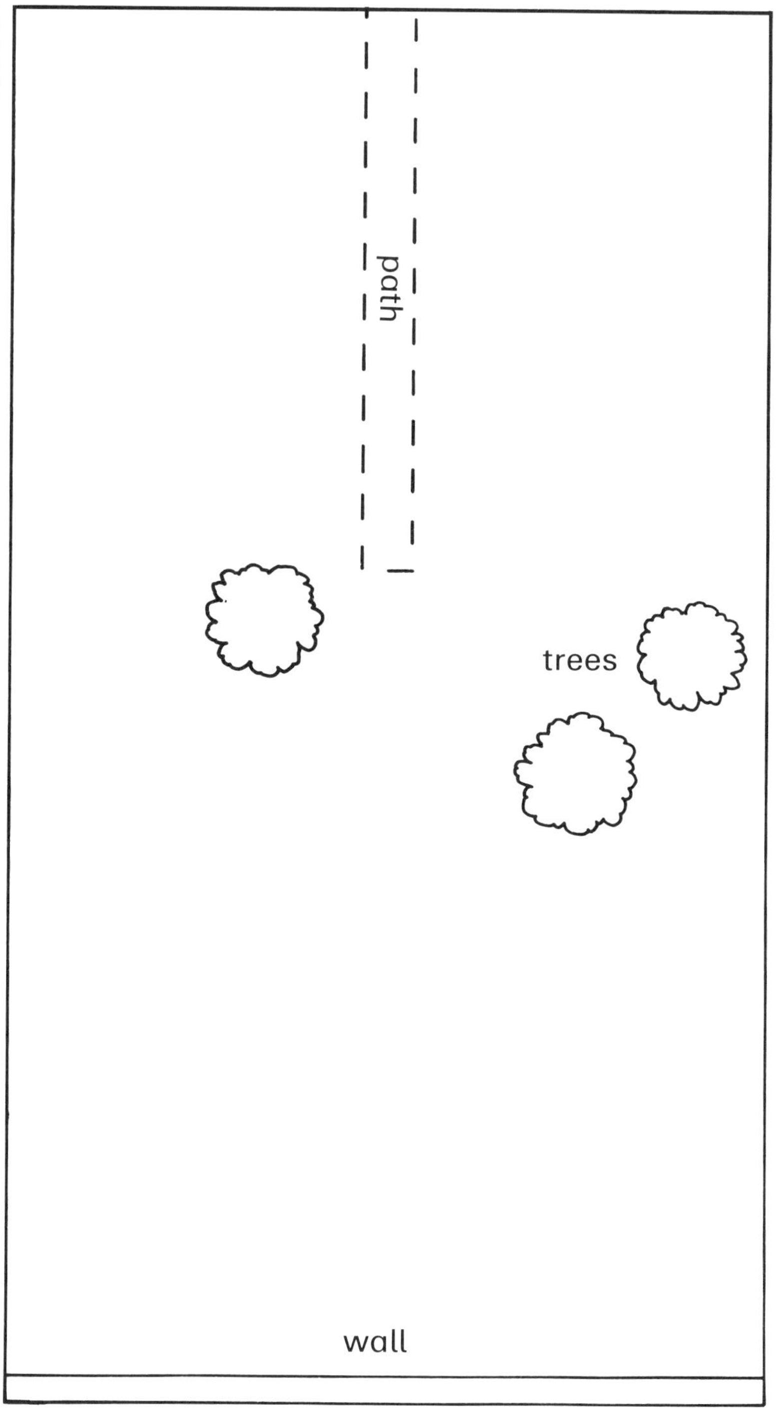

Name ______________________

Classroom measurements

Working from the plan, calculate the length of different journeys from table 5 to the places marked. Record your answer in the table below.

Plan of Class 5, St. Martin's Primary School

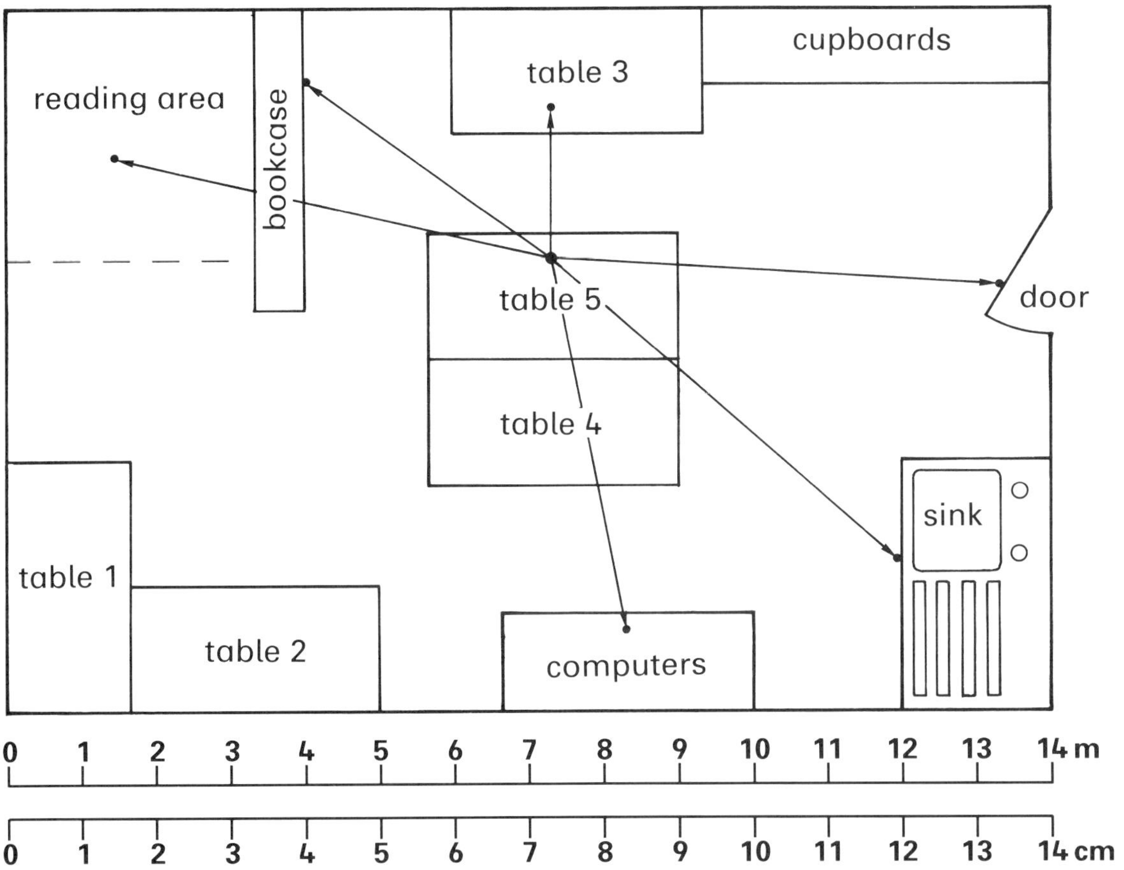

1 centimetre (cm) on the plan measures 1 metre (m) in the classroom.

Journey	Distance on plan	Real distance
Table 5 to table 3		
Table 5 to the door		
Table 5 to the reading area		
Table 5 to the computers		
Table 5 to the sink		
Table 5 to the bookcase		

Name ______________________________

Direction finder

1. Make a tracing of the 'direction finder' shown below.

2. Cut round the dotted lines and use your 'direction finder' with a map of your area.

Direction finder

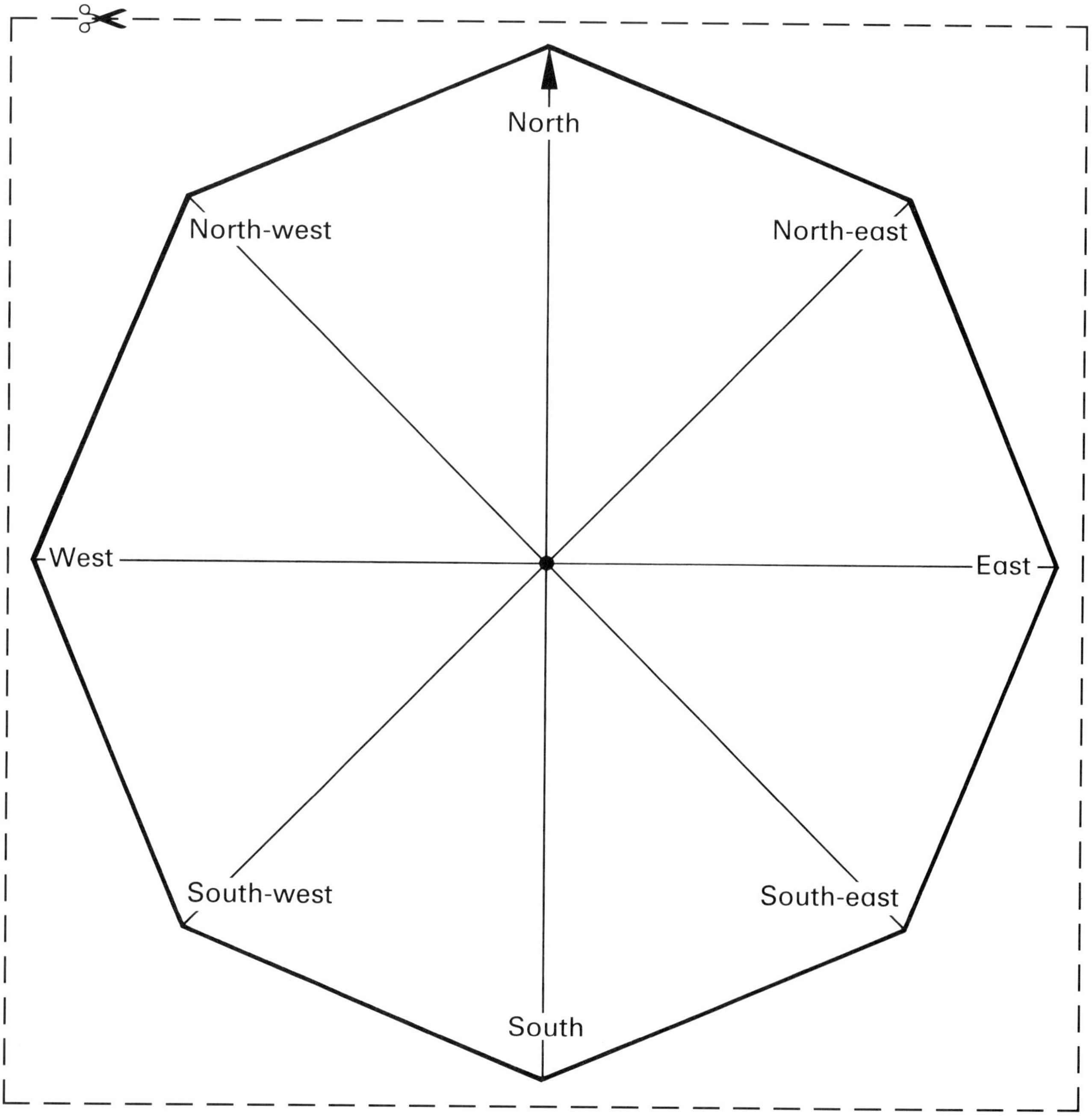

Name ________________________________

Barriers

1. Colour the key and the map of south-west England.

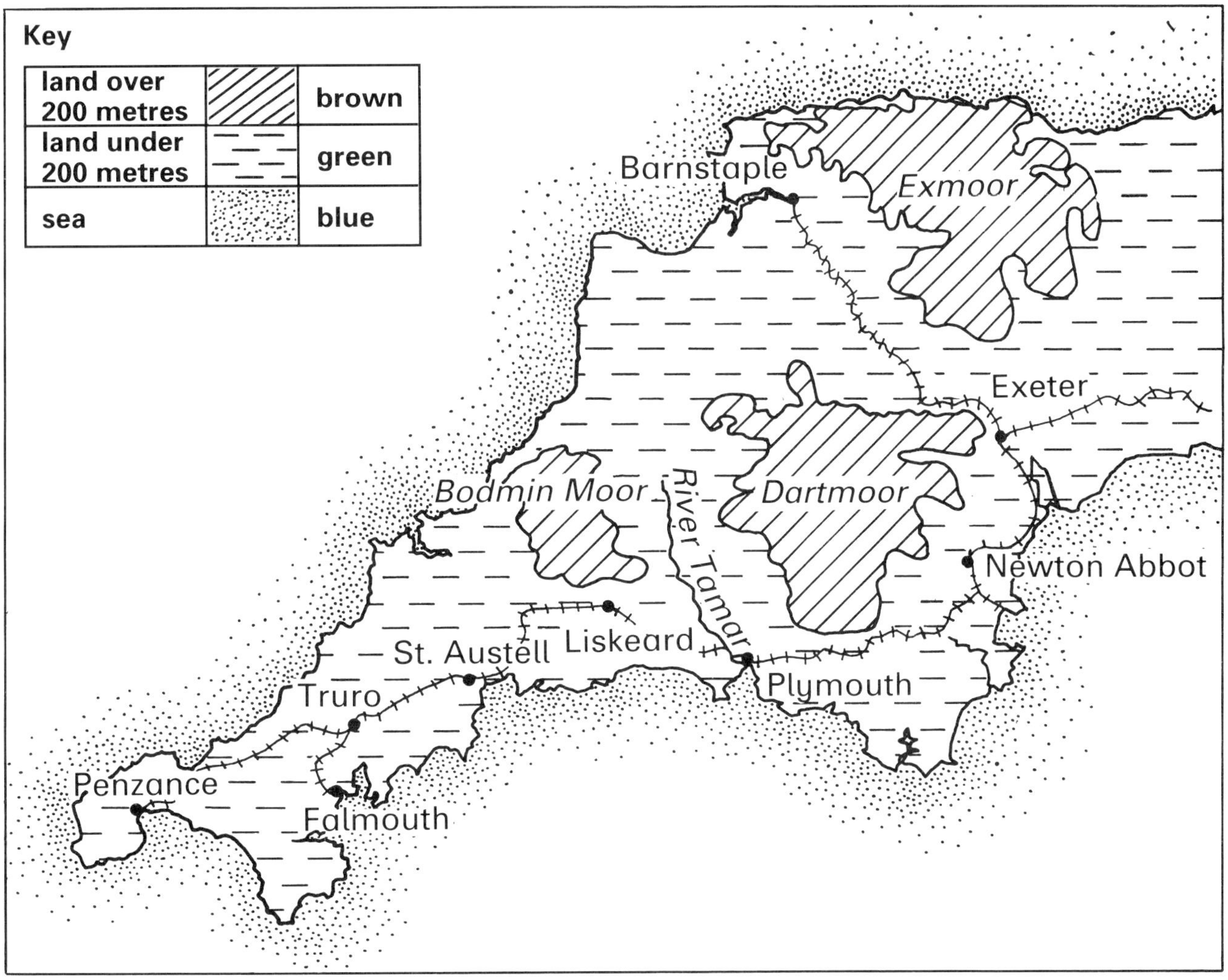

2. Draw a straight line from Falmouth to Exeter. Name three obstacles for the railway.

a ______________ b ______________ c ______________

3. Complete the diagram below by naming the towns along the route.

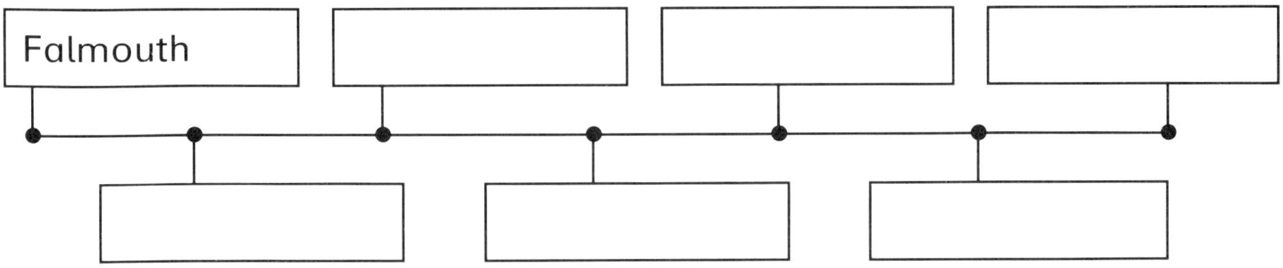

Name ______________________________

Scale bar

1. Draw straight lines linking London to the other cities marked on the map.
2. Calculate the distance from London to each city using the scale bar below. Write the answer in the table.
3. Write down the compass direction in the last column.

City	Distance from London	Compass direction

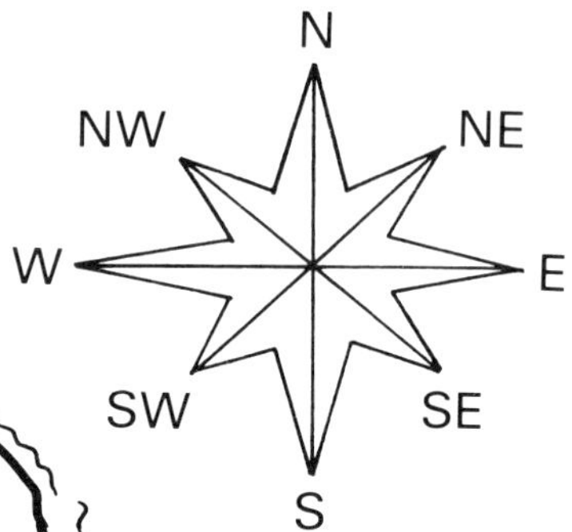

1 cm on the map measures 50 km on the ground.

Name ______________________________

School trail

Complete a box for each stop on the trail. Write down the number, describe the place, and say what you can see, hear, touch and do at the stop.

Stop ☐	Place ______________
see	
hear	
touch	
do	

Stop ☐	Place ______________
see	
hear	
touch	
do	

Stop ☐	Place ______________
see	
hear	
touch	
do	

Stop ☐	Place ______________
see	
hear	
touch	
do	

Name ____________________________

Different directions

1. Write the correct letters on the points of the compass below.

2. Make a list of countries in different compass directions from the British Isles.

North-east
1.
2.
3.

East
1.
2.
3.

South-east
1.
2.
3.

South
1.
2.
3.

South-west
1.
2.
3.

West
1.
2.

North-west
1.
2.

3. In which direction are there no countries at all? ____________________

Name ________________________________

Rivers and mountains

1. Working from the index of your atlas, find a map that shows the rivers listed in the tables below. Name three countries along the route, and also name the sea or ocean that each one flows into.

River Nile
1.
2.
3.
Flows into

River Amazon
1.
2.
3.
Flows into

River Rhine
1.
2.
3.
Flows into

River Indus
1.
2.
3.
Flows into

2. Now find a map of the mountains listed below, and name the mountain range to which they belong.

Mountain	Mountain range
Mount Everest	
Mont Blanc	
Aconcagua	
Mount McKinley	

Name ____________________________

Country profile

Draw a sketch map of the country and complete the datafile.

Sketch map

Theme	Information
rivers	
mountains	
climate	
main cities	
crops	
resources	
other information	

Name ______________________

Comparisons

1. Answer the following questions about the place where you live.

Questions	Answers
1. Do you live inland or on the coast?	
2. Do you live close to or away from mountains?	
3. Do you live in a village, town or city?	
4. Do the farmers mostly keep animals or mostly grow crops?	
5. Do you live less than or more than 100 km from London?	

2. Name a place in the United Kingdom that you have visited.

____

3. Now answer the following questions about this place using an atlas to help you.

Questions	Answers
1. Is it inland or on the coast?	
2. Is it close to or away from mountains?	
3. Is it a village, town or city?	
4. Do the farmers mostly keep animals or mostly grow crops?	
5. Is it less than or more than 100 km from London?	

4. Write a few sentences on a separate piece of paper about how the two places compare.

Name ______________________________

Continent Cube

1. Colour the continent shapes.
2. Cut round the edge of the cube.
3. Fold along the lines and glue down the flaps to make your model.

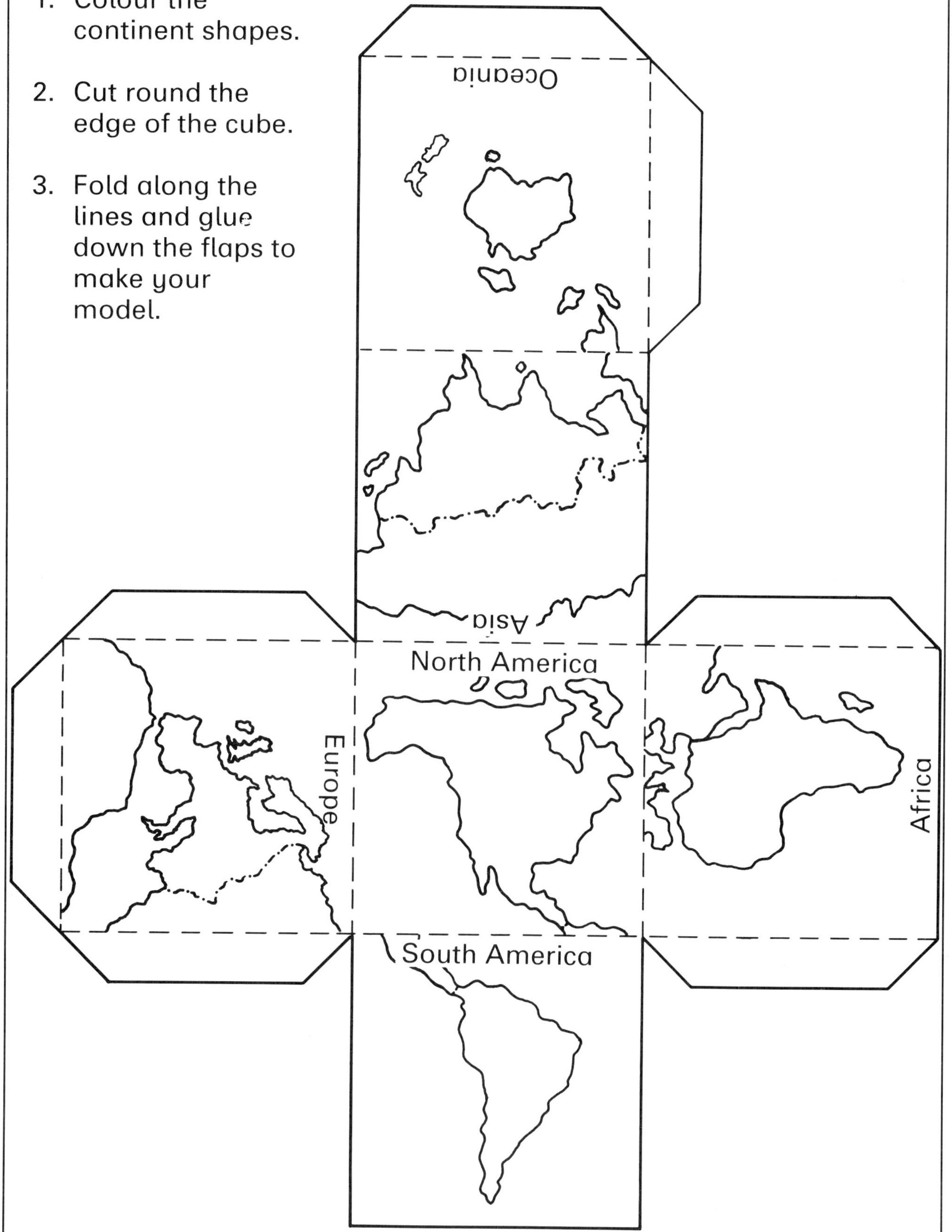

Name ______________________________

UK mountains and rivers

1. Colour the key.
2. Colour the map in the same way, and fill in the names of the rivers and mountains.

Key

mountains	
rivers	
sea	

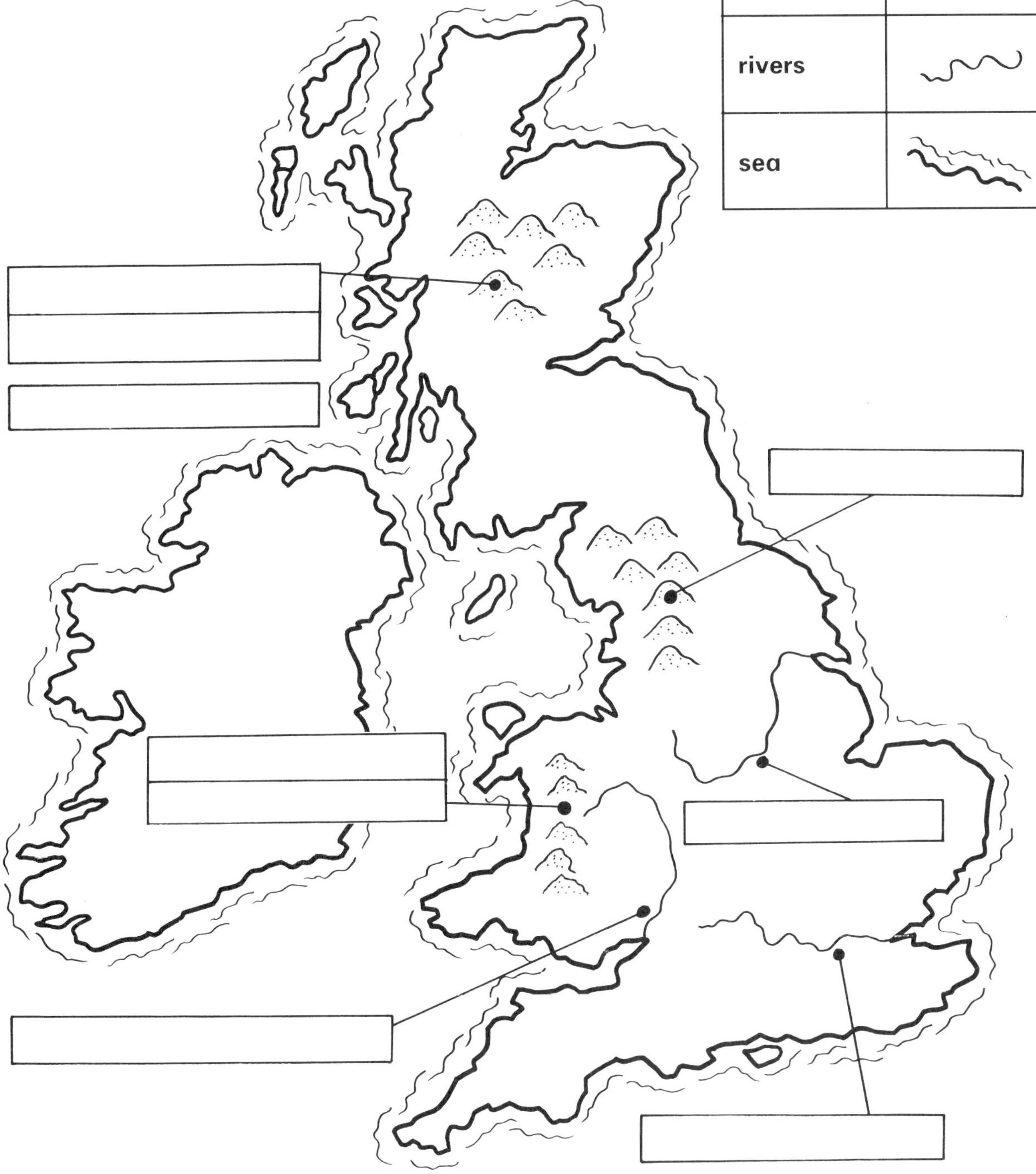

Name ______________________________

United Kingdom countries and capitals

1. Colour the outline shape of the shaded countries.
2. Name each country and its capital city.

Country ______________________

Capital ______________________

Country ______________________

Capital ______________________

Country ______________________

Capital ______________________

Country ______________________

____

Capital ______________________

Name ______________________________

United Kingdom

1. Colour each of the country shapes below.
2. Carefully cut them out and make the pieces into a map of the British Isles.
3. Glue them down on to a separate piece of paper.

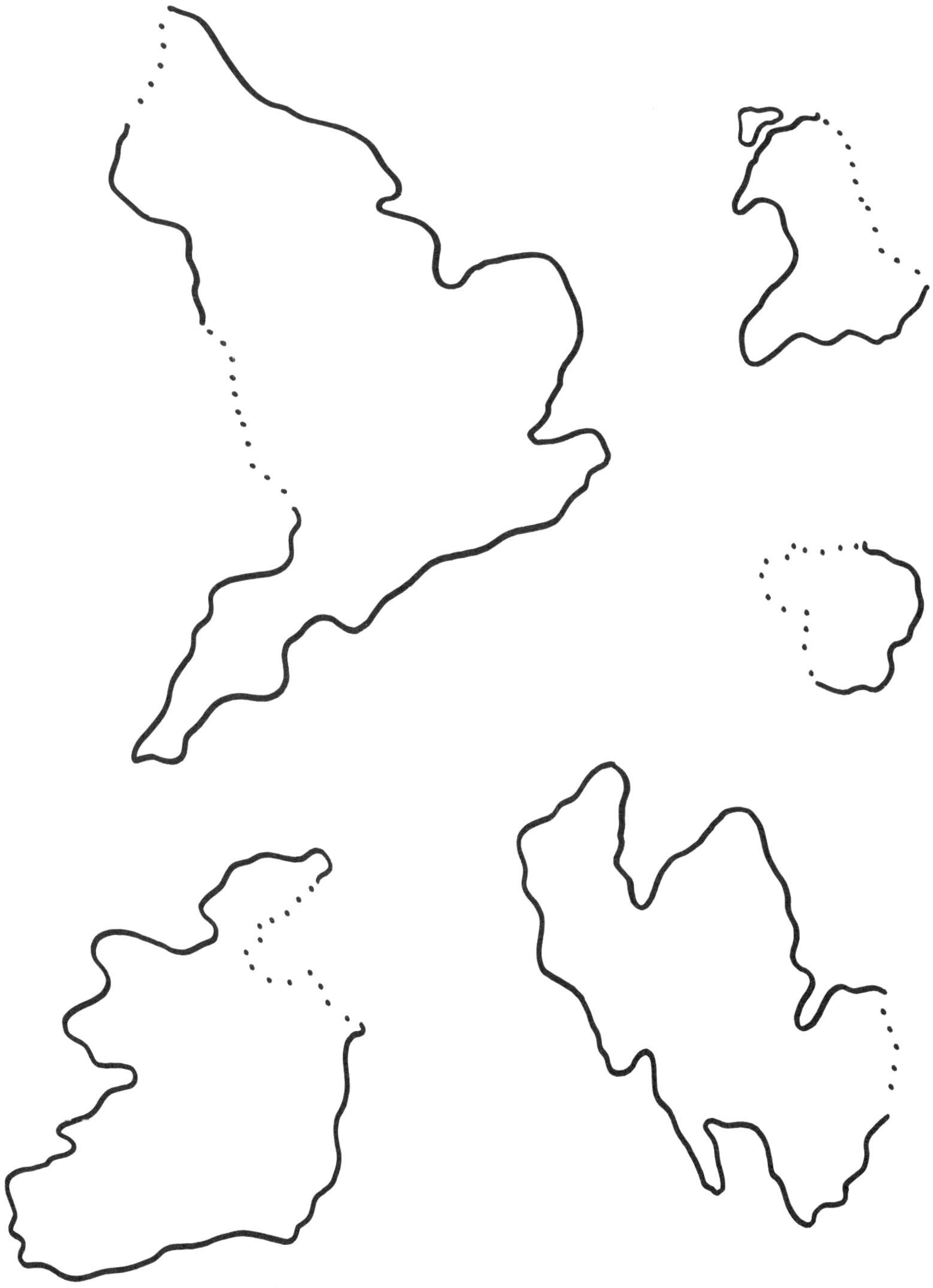

Name ______________________________

Railway routes

1. Working from an atlas, draw the railway routes on the map as carefully as possible.
2. Name one major obstacle which prevents each route from following a completely straight line.

Route
London to Plymouth
Obstacle

Route
London to Fishguard
Obstacle

Route
London to Glasgow
Obstacle

Route
London to Aberdeen
Obstacle

Route
London to Calais
Obstacle

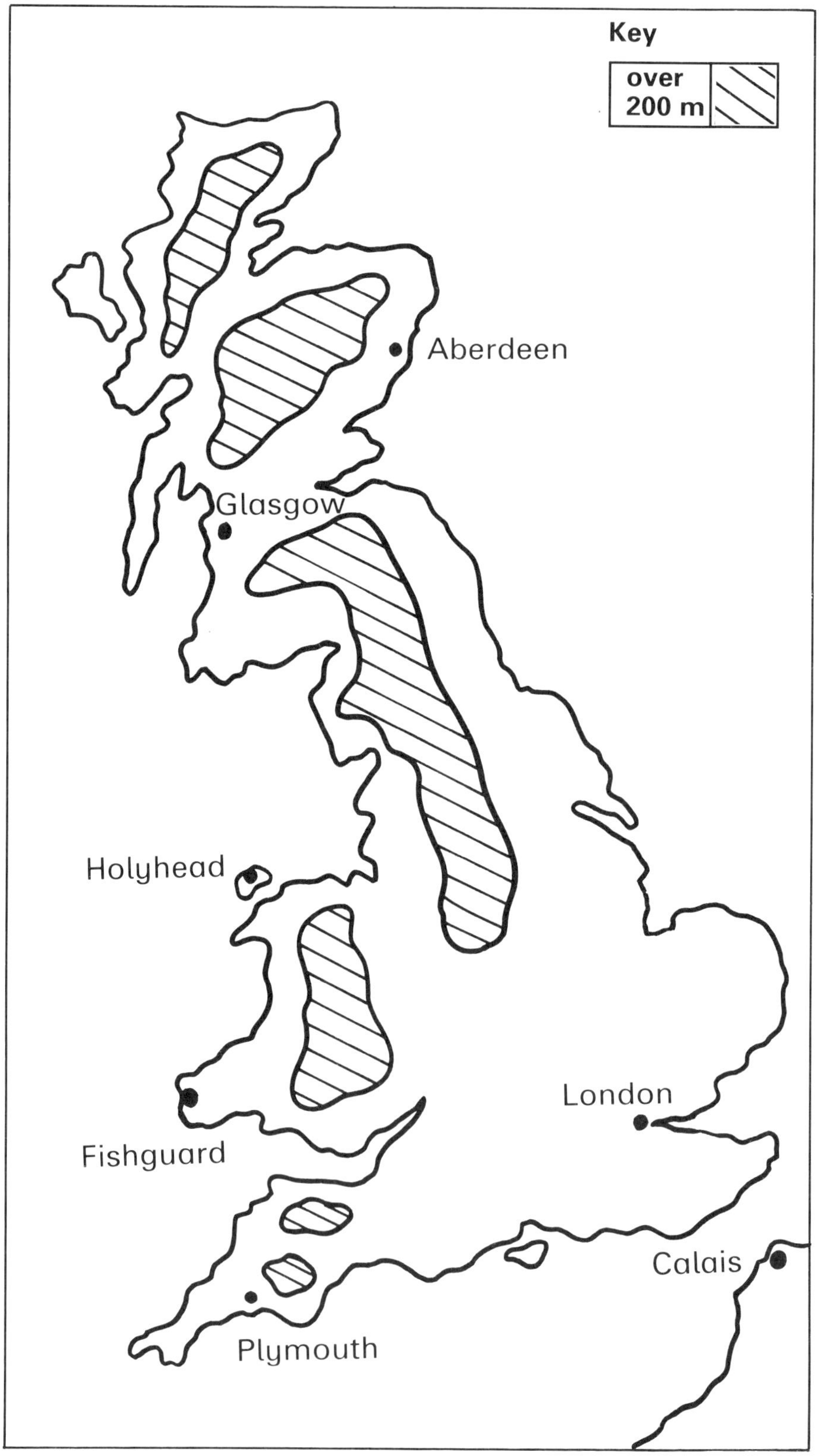

Name ____________________________

Motorway routes

1. Using an atlas to help you, name the motorways shown on the map. Add each motorway number carefully on to the map.

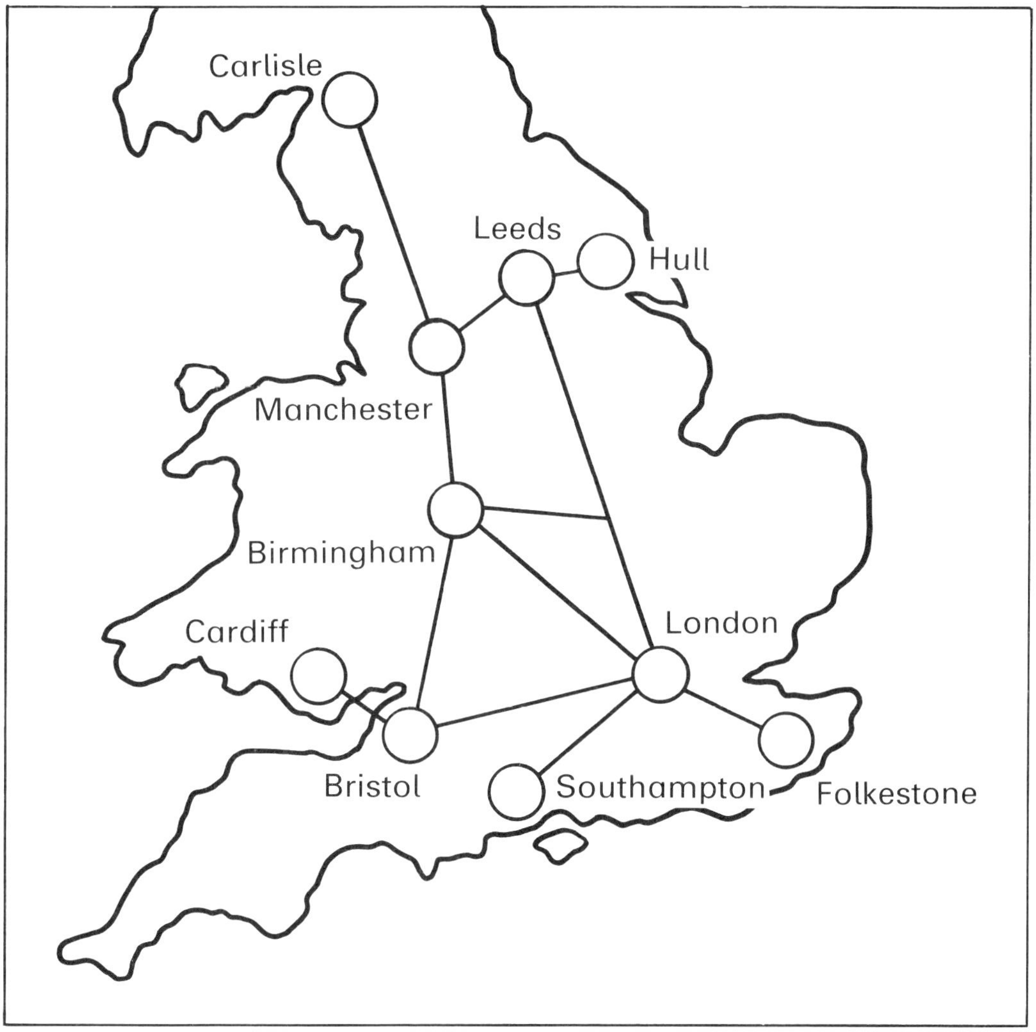

2. Write down in the empty circles how many motorways leave each place.

3. Write each place in the correct part of the diagram below.

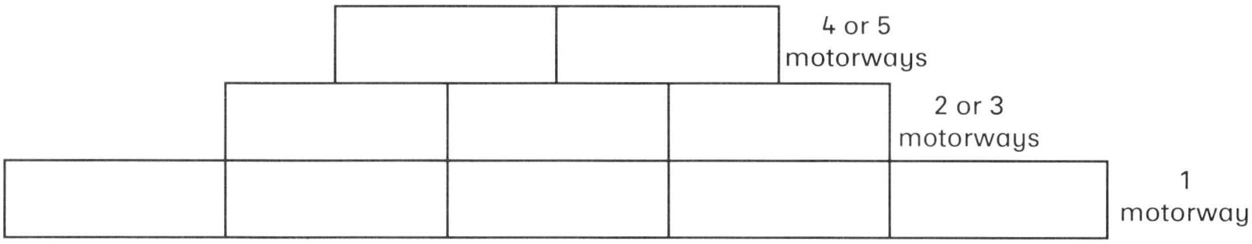

4. Which places have the best motorway links?

____

Name ______________________________

European capitals

1. Colour the code boxes in the key.
2. Colour the countries on the map using this code.
3. Name the capital city of each country.
4. Using the scale bar, estimate the distance from London to each of the other capitals.

Country	Code	Capital	Distance from London
UK	red		
France	green		
Spain	blue		
Germany	brown		
Italy	yellow		

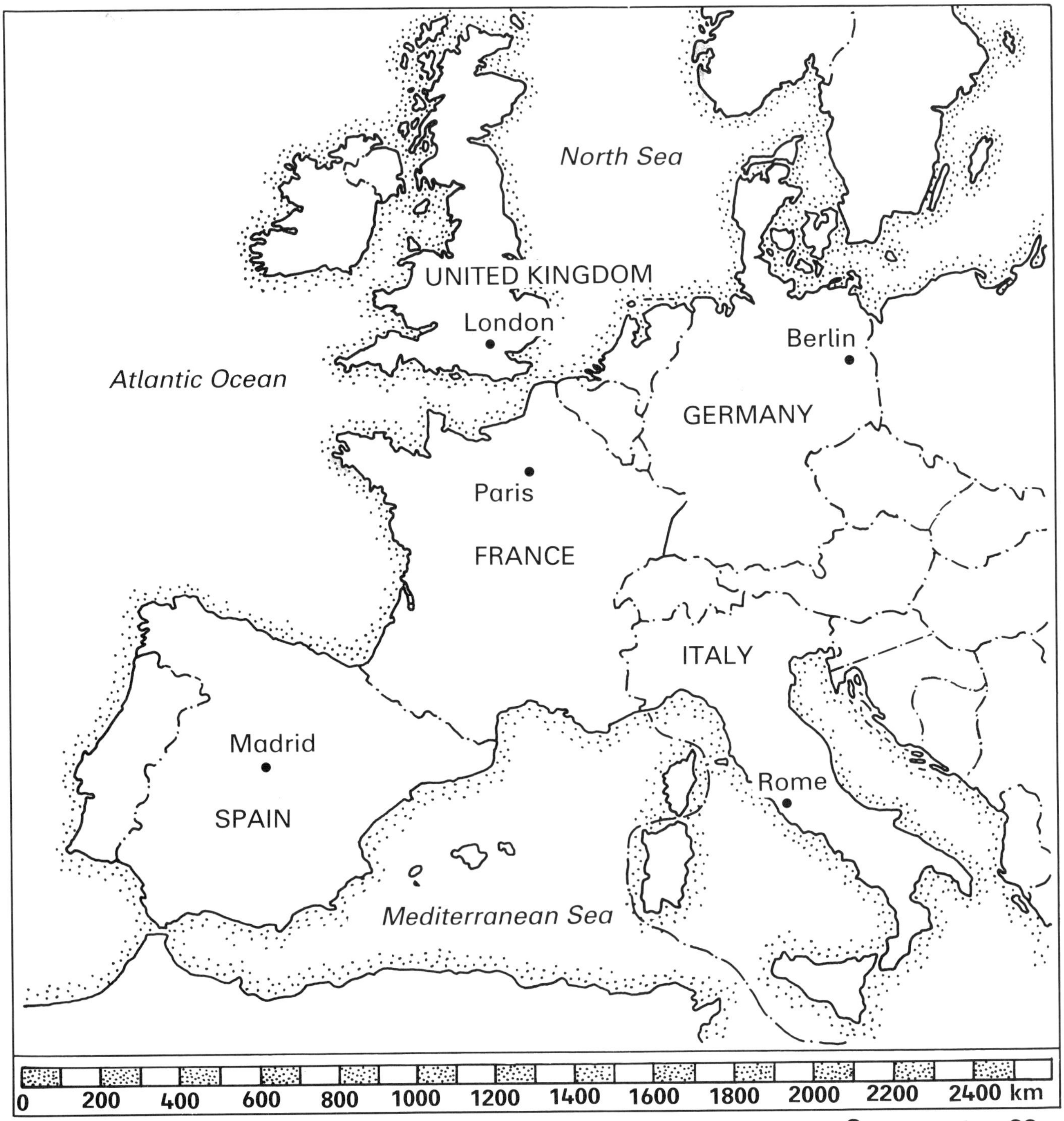

Name ______________________________

European countries

1. Colour the countries shown on the maps.
2. Name each one using an atlas to help you.

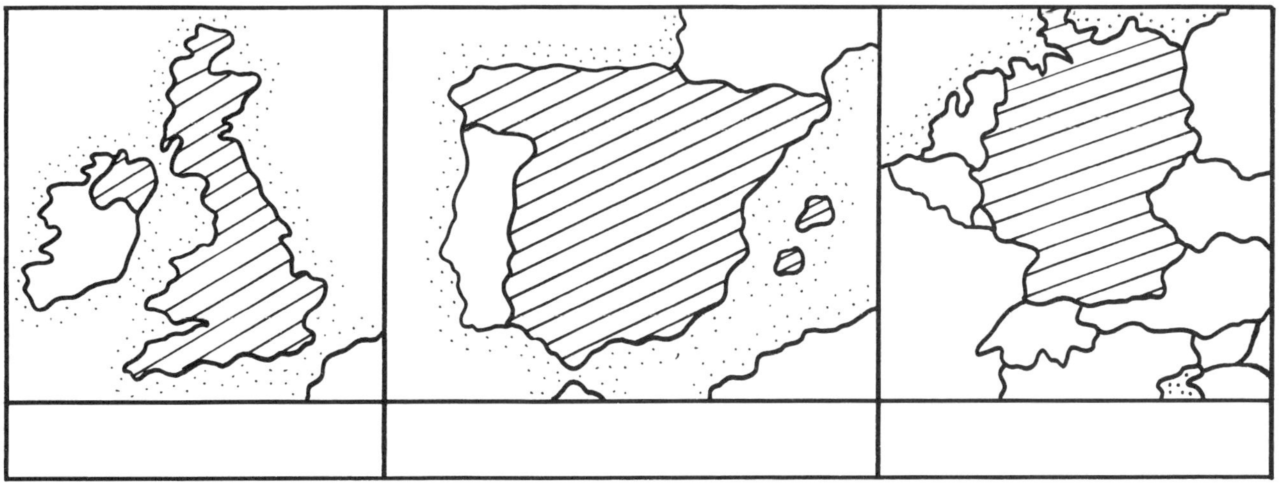

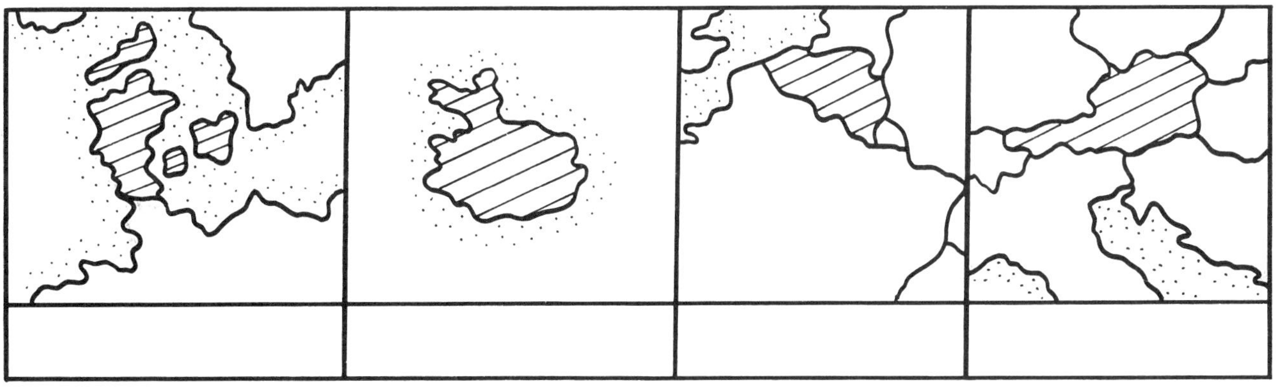

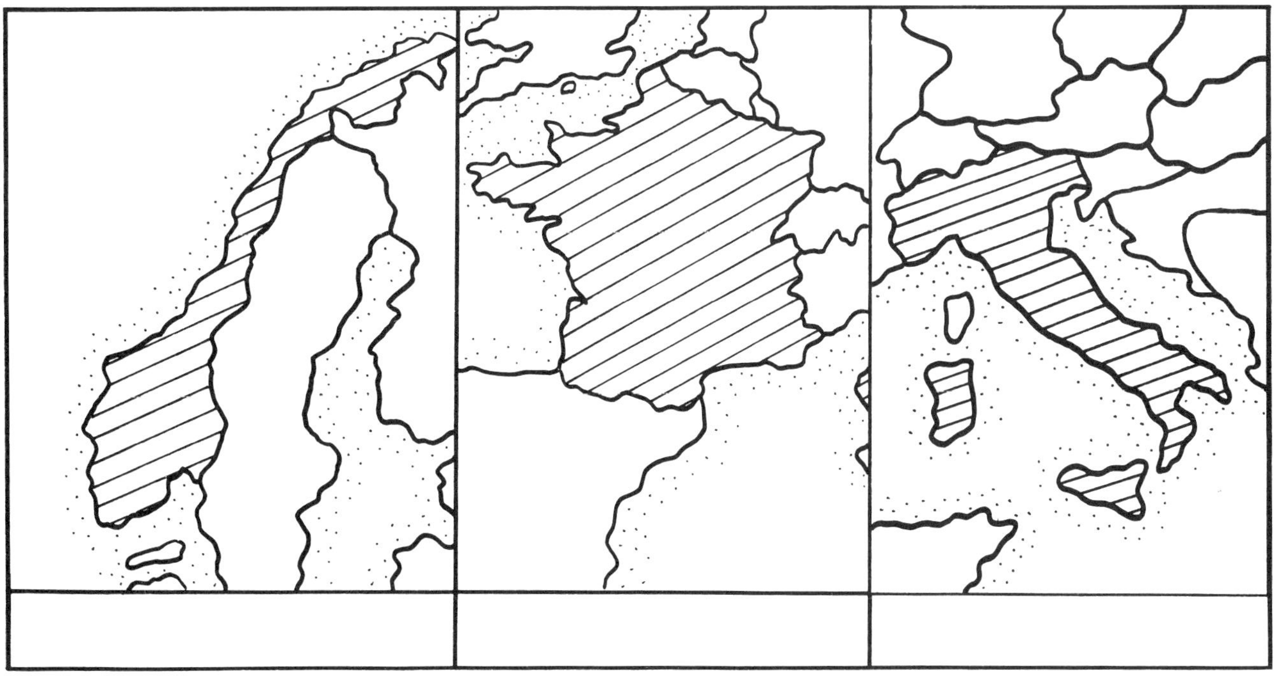

Name ____________________

World mountains, rivers and deserts

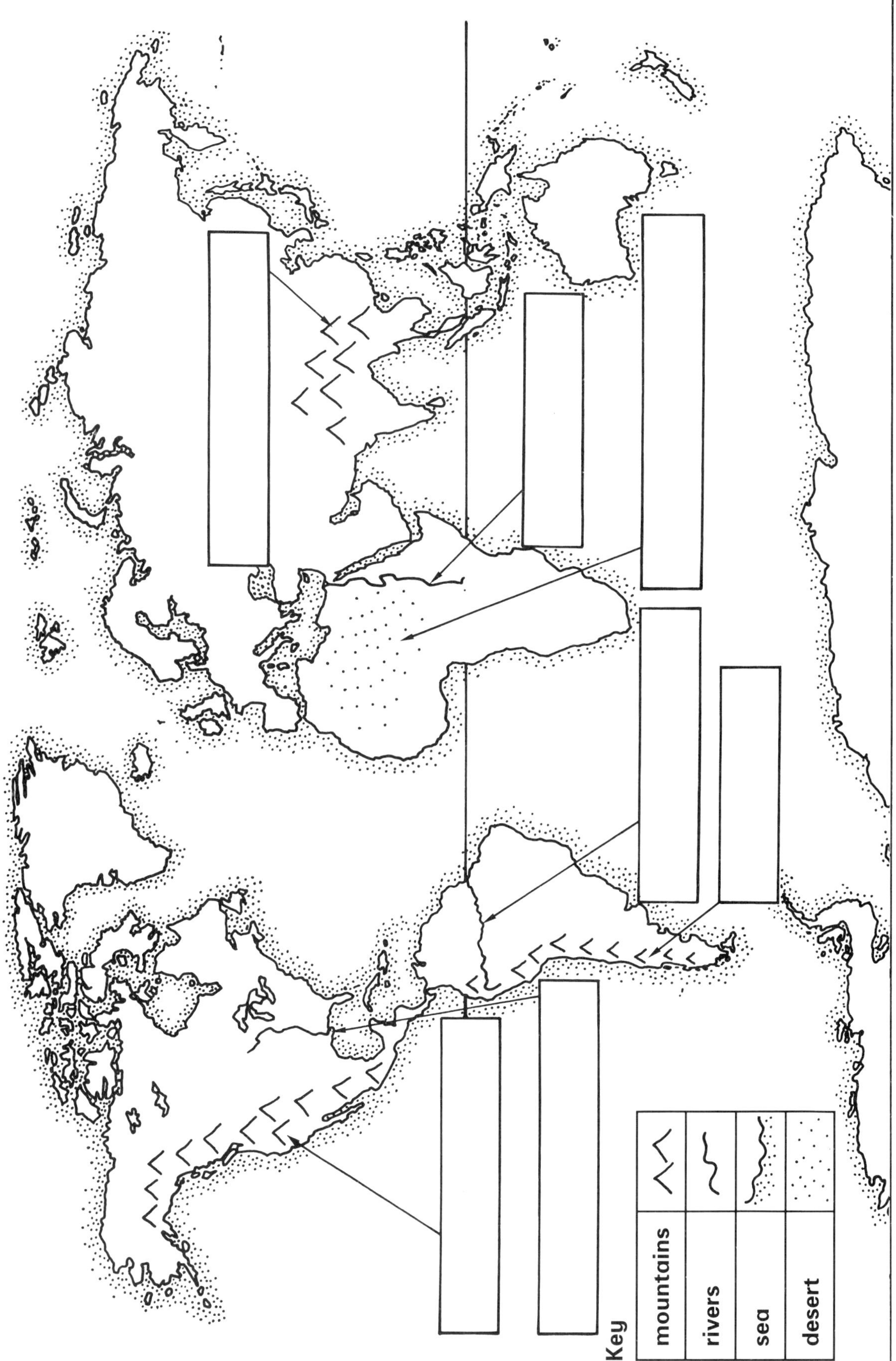

1. Colour the key.
2. Name the mountains, rivers and deserts.
3. Colour the map in the same way as the key.

Name ______________________________

World countries

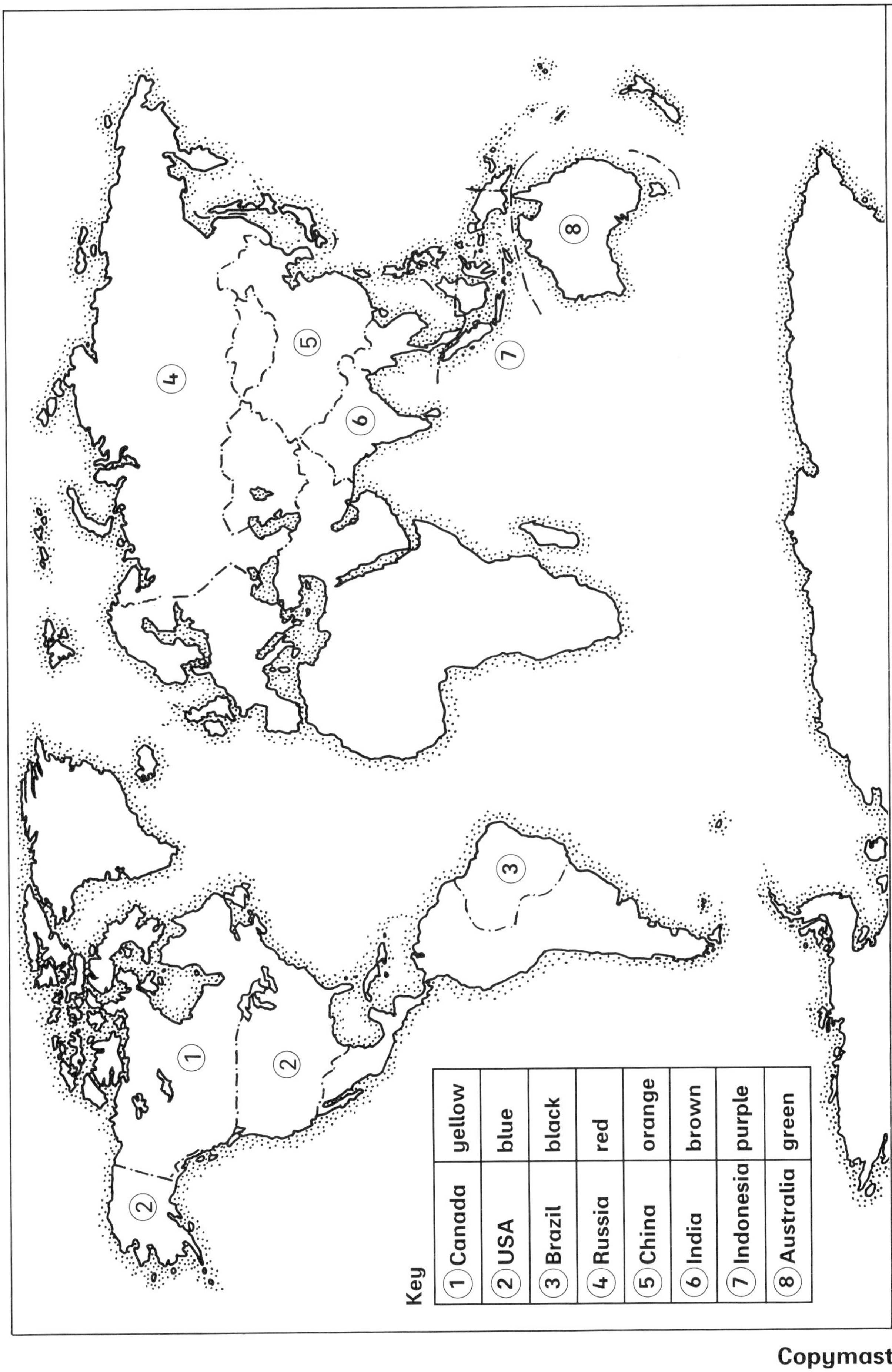

Key

① Canada	yellow
② USA	blue
③ Brazil	black
④ Russia	red
⑤ China	orange
⑥ India	brown
⑦ Indonesia	purple
⑧ Australia	green

1. Colour the code boxes in the key.
2. Colour the countries on the map in the same way.

Name ________________________________

Places worldwide

Column A

Continents	Spell correctly?	Find on map?
North America		
South America		
Europe		
Africa		
Asia		
Oceania		
Antarctica		
Oceans	Spell correctly?	Find on map?
Arctic Ocean		
Atlantic Ocean		
Pacific Ocean		
Indian Ocean		
Mountains/deserts	Spell correctly?	Find on map?
Rocky Mountains		
Andes		
Himalayas		
Sahara Desert		
Canals	Spell correctly?	Find on map?
Panama Canal		
Suez Canal		

Column B

Countries	Spell correctly?	Find on map?
Canada		
USA		
Brazil		
Russia		
India		
China		
Indonesia		
Australia		
Cities	Spell correctly?	Find on map?
New York		
Buenos Aires		
Paris		
Cairo		
Bombay		
Sydney		
Rivers/seas	Spell correctly?	Find on map?
Mississippi		
Amazon		
Nile		
Caribbean Sea		

Name ______________________

School address

Use an envelope addressed to your school to help you complete the diagram below.

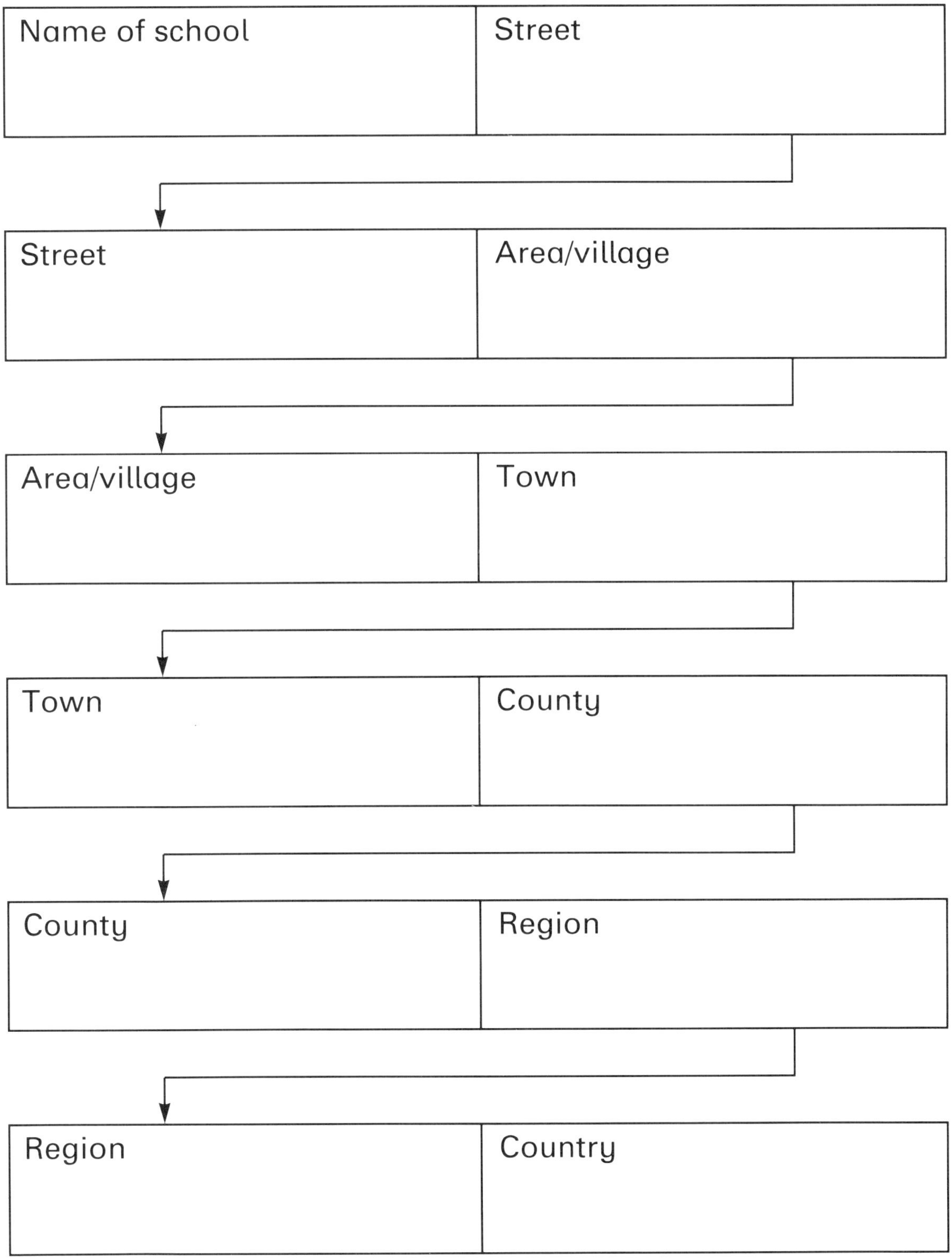

Name ______________________________

Weather profile

Draw a weather profile on the chart below. First fill in the empty boxes, then join the correct points in each line and colour the shape you have made.

Date

Time

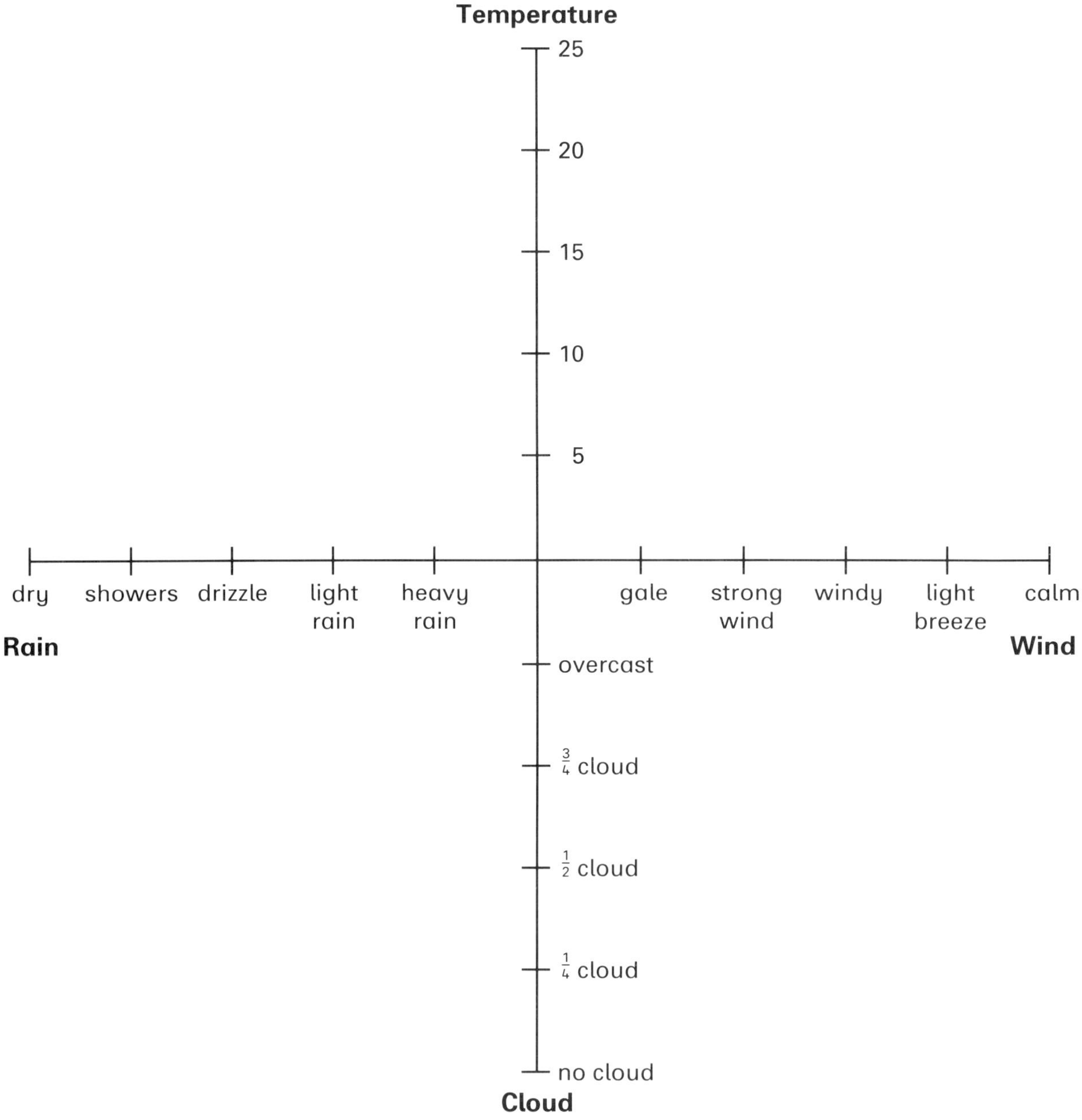

Place

Region of the United Kingdom

Name ______________________________

Wet and dry

1. Colour the code boxes in the table below. This tells you how quickly surfaces dry out.

Surface	Description	Colour code
roof and walls	dry very fast	red
tarmac and paving stones	dry quite fast	yellow
grass and flower beds	dry rather slowly	green
pond	never dries out	blue

2. Now colour the plan of St. Peter's Primary School using the colours from the colour code.

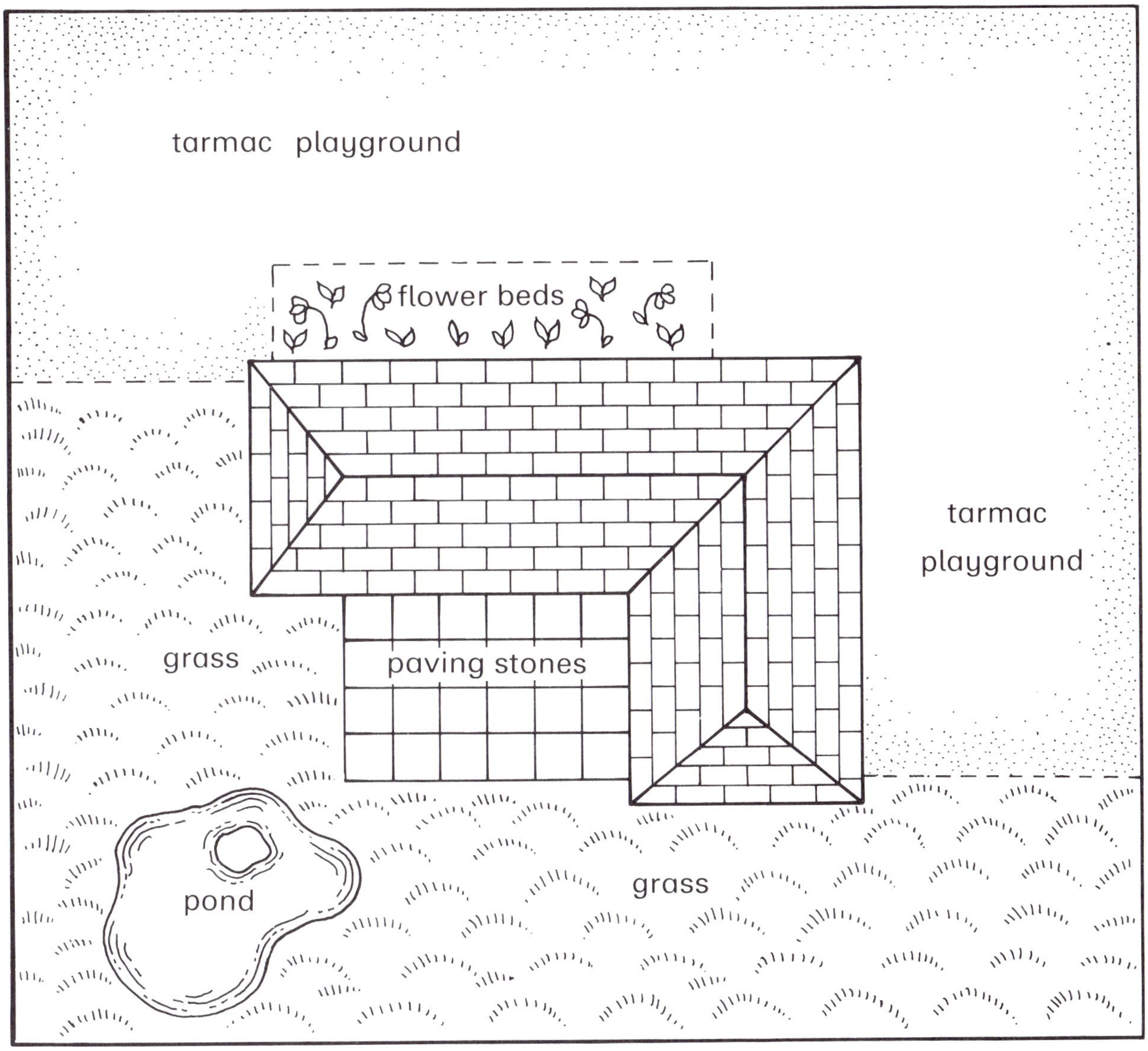

3. Make a similar survey of your own school.

Name ______________________________

Street furniture

1. Make a list of the things you need to consider when choosing a site for each item of street furniture listed below.
2. Identify some suitable places on a map of your area.

New bottle bank 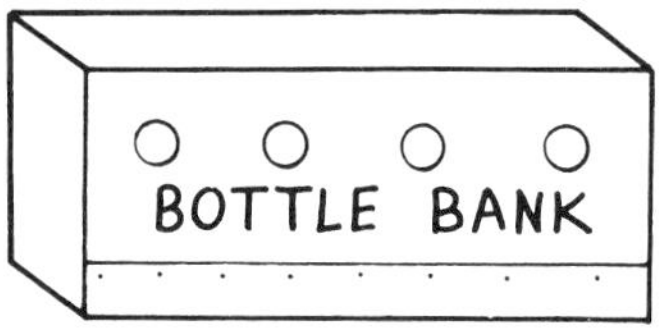
1.
2.
3.
4.

New seat 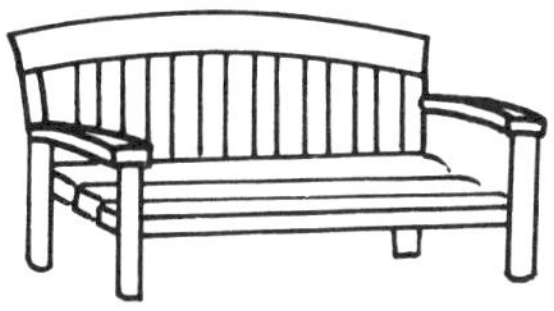
1.
2.
3.
4.

New bus stop 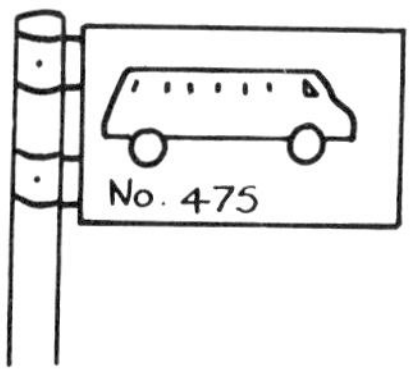
1.
2.
3.
4.

New safety barrier 
1.
2.
3.
4.

Name ______________________________

New schemes

1. Consider the different schemes listed in the table and decide how you would rank them in order of preference. Begin by writing your name in the empty space. Then record your opinion by putting 1 under your first choice, 2 under your second choice and so on, finally putting a seven under your last choice.

2. Record in the same way what six other children in your class think.

	Scheme						
Name	shopping centre	skating rink	picnic area	adventure playground	butterfly garden	sports centre	fast-food restaurant
Total							

3. Add up the totals.

4. Which scheme seems most popular (has the lowest score)?

____

5. Can you explain why it is needed?

____

____

Name ______________________________

Impact studies

1. Find out about four different projects which are planned for your area.

2. Describe the projects in the table below and list the advantages and disadvantages.

Project	Advantages	Disadvantages

3. Which project do you think is best? ______________________

Name ______________________________

Plan a village

Design a village by drawing symbols from the key on the map.
You can use each symbol as many times as you want.

Key

old church

old house

inn

shop

new houses

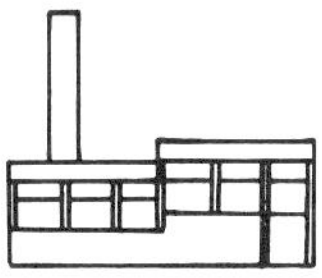

school

petrol station

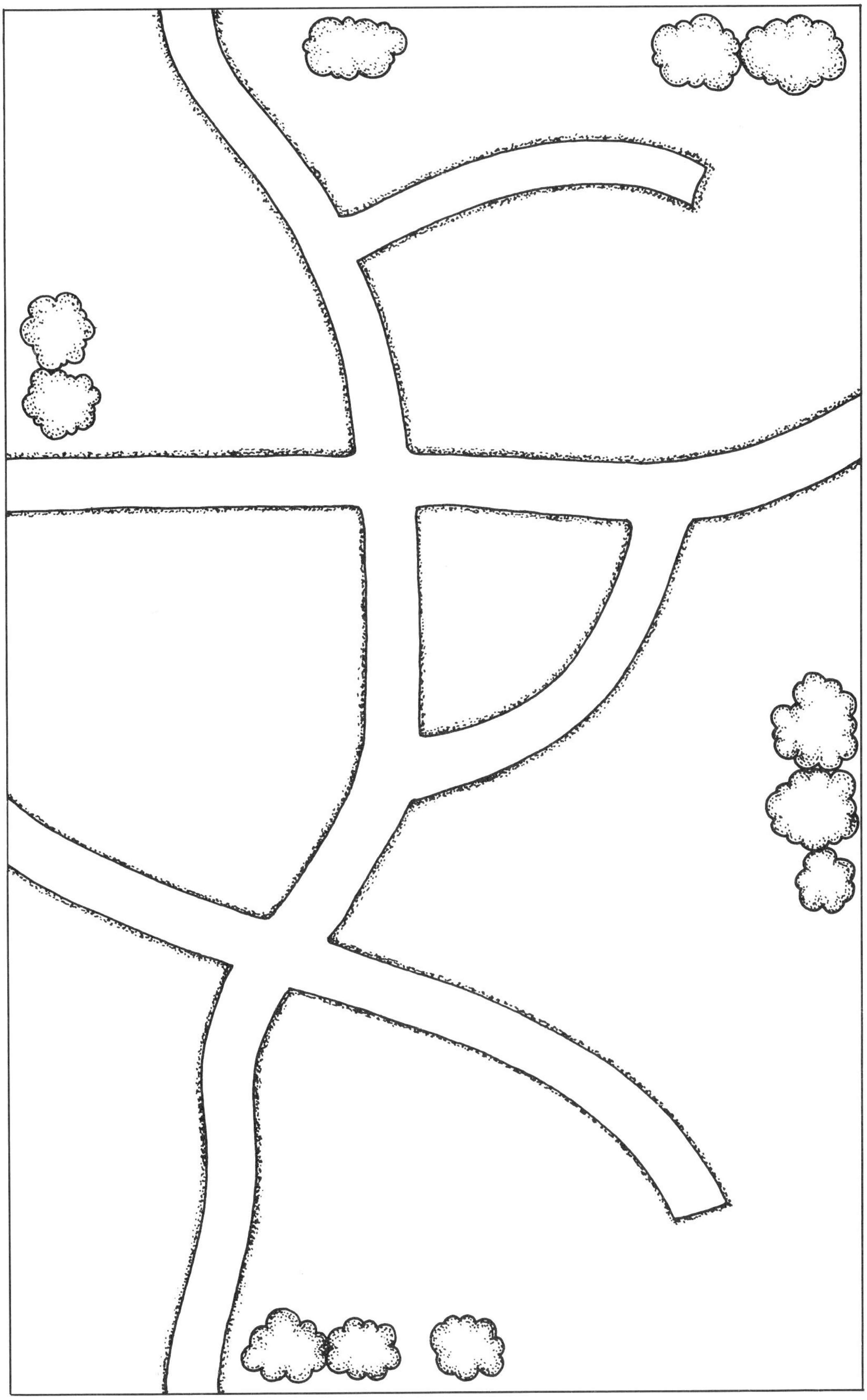

Name ________________________________

Different Places

Colton – Staffordshire

Swansea – West Glamorgan

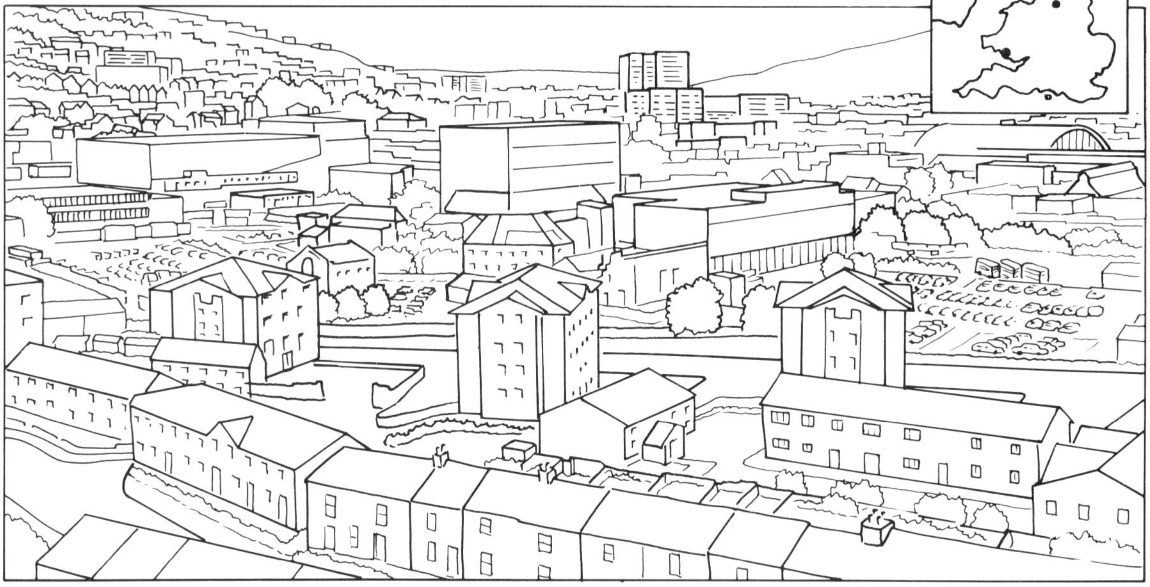

1. Colour the two pictures.

2. Make a list of the main differences between Colton and Swansea.

	Colton	Swansea
Landscape		
Buildings		
Transport		

Name ________________________________

Best place

1. Ask twelve children in your class the following two questions:
   Would you prefer to live in the town or country?
   Would you prefer to live in the United Kingdom or abroad?
   Show their answers by putting a tick or cross in the table.

Name of child	Town	Country	UK	Abroad
Total number of ticks				

2. Add up the totals.
3. Tick the boxes to complete the sentences below.

The survey shows most children would prefer to live a) in the town ☐
b) in the country. ☐

The survey shows most children would prefer to live a) in the UK ☐
b) abroad. ☐

Name ______________________________

Connections

1. Write down the towns within 10 and 20 miles by main road of
   (a) your local area
   (b) the contrasting locality that you are studying.

Local Area

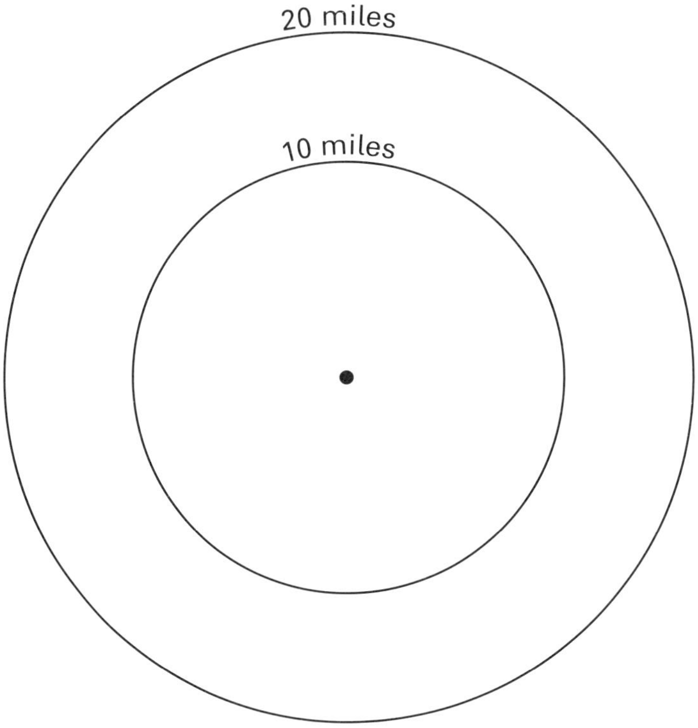

Contrasting Locality

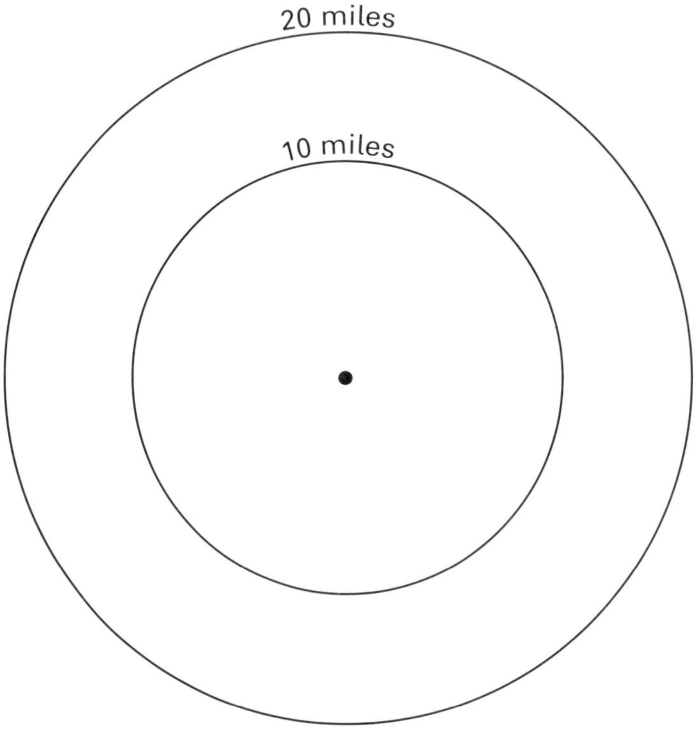

Name ______________________________

Questions

Answer these questions about the place you are studying. You may need to say 'none' in some cases.

Landscape

Is it an island or part of the mainland?	
What is the name of the nearest river?	
What is the name of the nearest mountain?	

Climate

Is it cold or hot, wet or dry?	
What problems does the weather cause?	

Settlement

Is it crowded or empty?	
What are the main towns?	

Work

How do people earn a living?	
What crops do farmers grow?	
What are the main industries?	

Transport

How do people move about?	
How are goods sent from place to place?	

Issues

How are things changing?	
What are the main environmental problems?	
What plans are there for the future?	

Name ________________________________

Differences in wealth

1. The table opposite tells you how much people earn on average in different cities around the world. Colour the code box red if they earn over £5 000 a year. Colour it yellow if they earn less than £5 000.
2. Name the cities on the map.
3. Colour each region the correct colour.

City	Region	Income	Code
New York	North America	£12 000	
Sao Paulo	South America	£1500	
Cairo	Africa	£400	
Paris	Europe	£10 000	
Moscow	North Asia	£1200	
Delhi	South Asia	£200	
Tehran	Middle East	£900	
Sydney	Australia	£10 000	

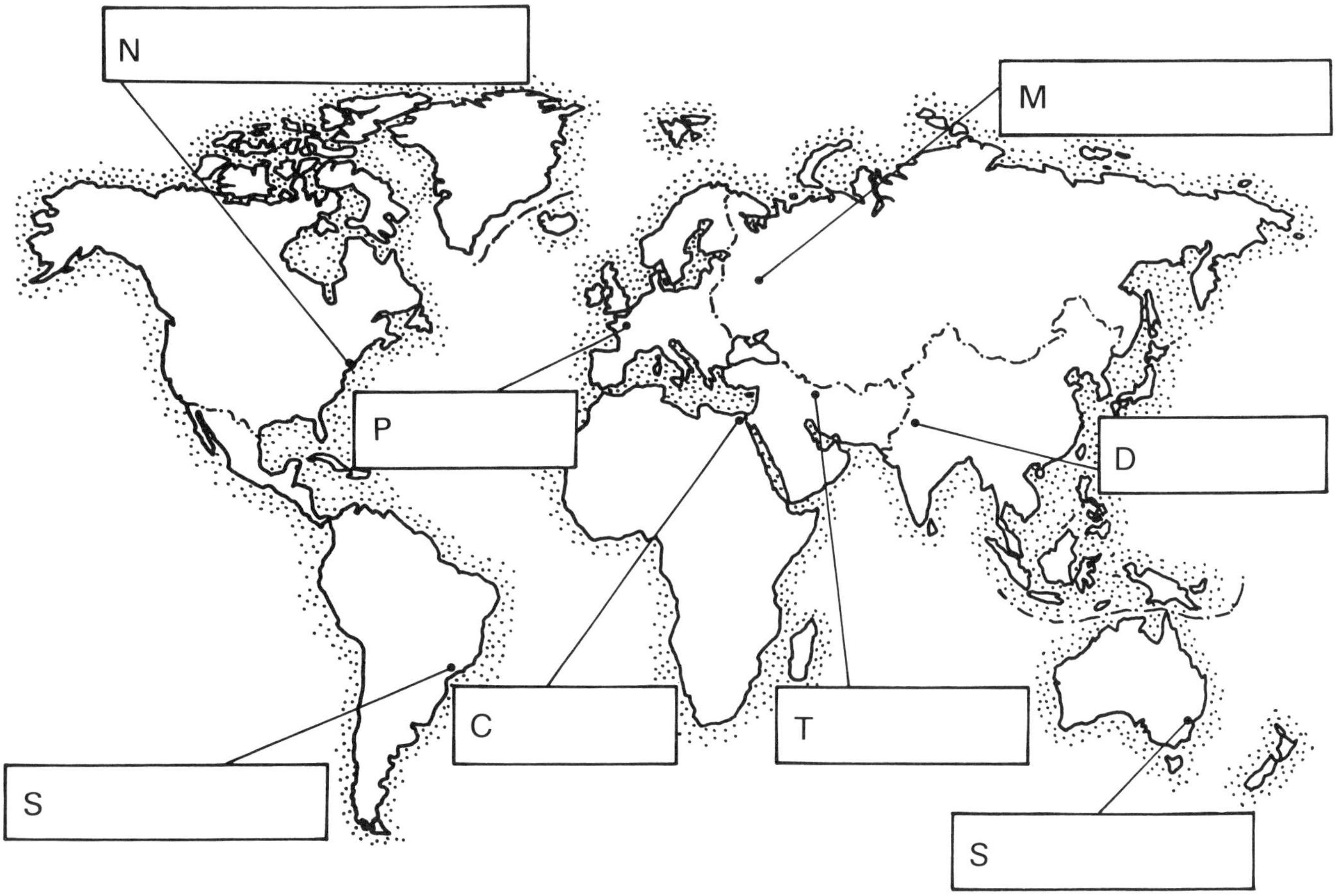

Name ______________________________

River systems

1. Colour the pictures.
2. Write a short sentence describing each feature of the river system.

source

tributaries

waterfall

meander

lake

mouth

Name ______________________________

Water symbols

1. Look at an Ordnance Survey map of your area.
2. Find an example of each of the features in the table.
3. Make your own coloured drawings in the empty spaces and add the local name.

Map feature	Name	Local example and name
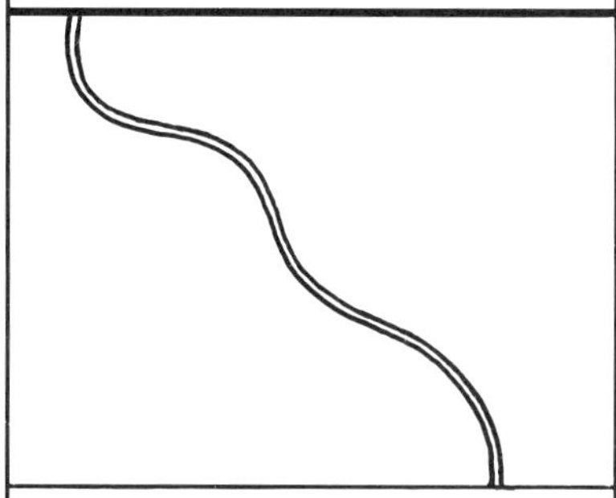	river	
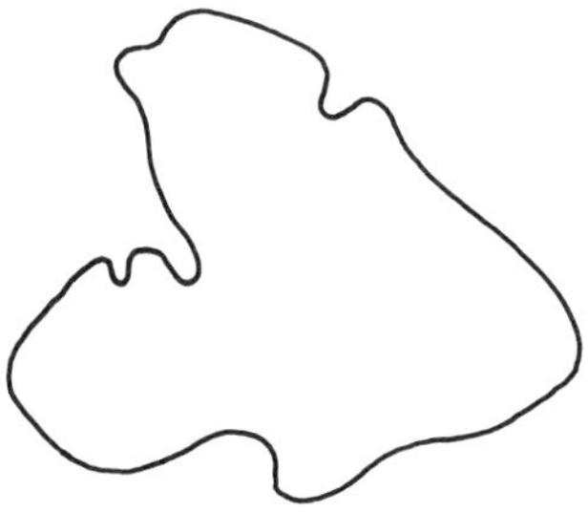	lake	
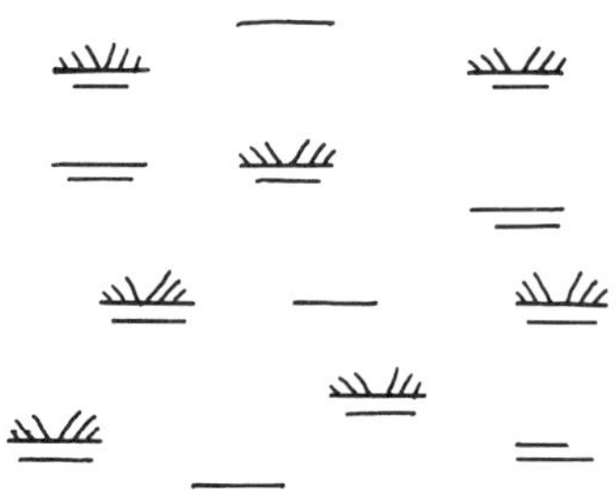	marsh	
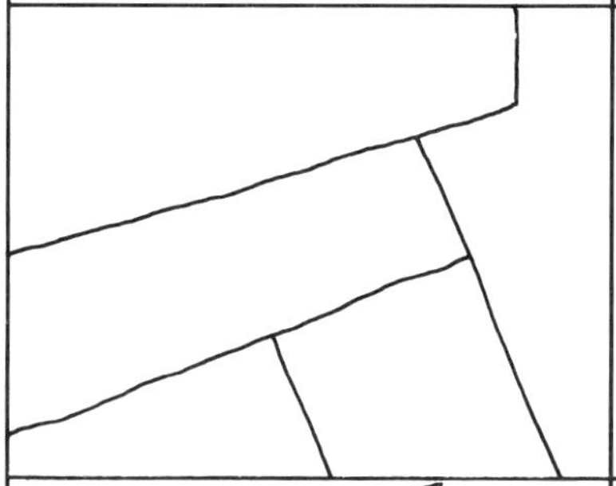	drainage ditches	
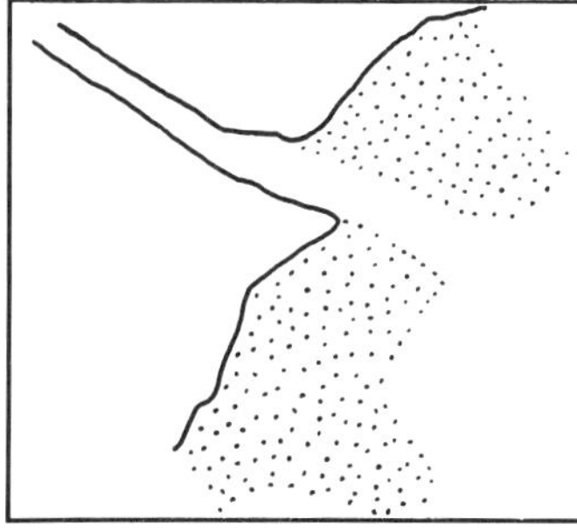	estuary and mudflats	

Name ______________________________

Rivers worldwide

1. Find the rivers listed in the table on an atlas map.
2. Name the sea or ocean that each one flows into.

River	Sea or ocean it flows into
Amazon	
Zambezi	
Mississippi	
Zaire	
Yenisei	
Volga	
St Lawrence	
Murray	
Colorado	
Yangtze	
Nile	
Ganges	

Name ______________________________

Wear and tear

1. Make a list of twenty things in and around your school that show signs of damage.
2. For each thing decide if the damage is due to human action or natural causes. Tick the correct box.
3. Think about the damage from natural causes. Tick the boxes to show if it is the result of wind, water or sun and frost.

Damage	**Human action**	**Natural causes**	**Natural causes**		
			Wind	Water	Sun/ Frost
Totals					

4. Which natural process seems to cause the most damage?

____

Name ______________________________

Local landscapes

1. Look at the different landscape features listed in the table. Tick if the feature is found locally.
2. Write down the local name of the features you have ticked.
3. Fill in the empty box at the foot of the table if your area has another landscape feature.

Landscape feature	✓	Local name
mountain		
hill		
valley		
river		
lowland		
lake		
seashore		

Name ______________________________

World landscapes

1. Working from an atlas, find out the names of mountains, rivers, lakes, islands and deserts around the world.
2. List them in the datafiles.

Mountains

Rivers

Lakes

Islands

Deserts

Name ______________________________

Deltas

1. Working from the list below, write the name of the river deltas in the spaces around the map.

1. Mississippi
2. Danube
3. Ganges
4. Huang Ho
5. Amazon
6. Niger
7. Nile
8. Mekong

1.	2.	3.	4.

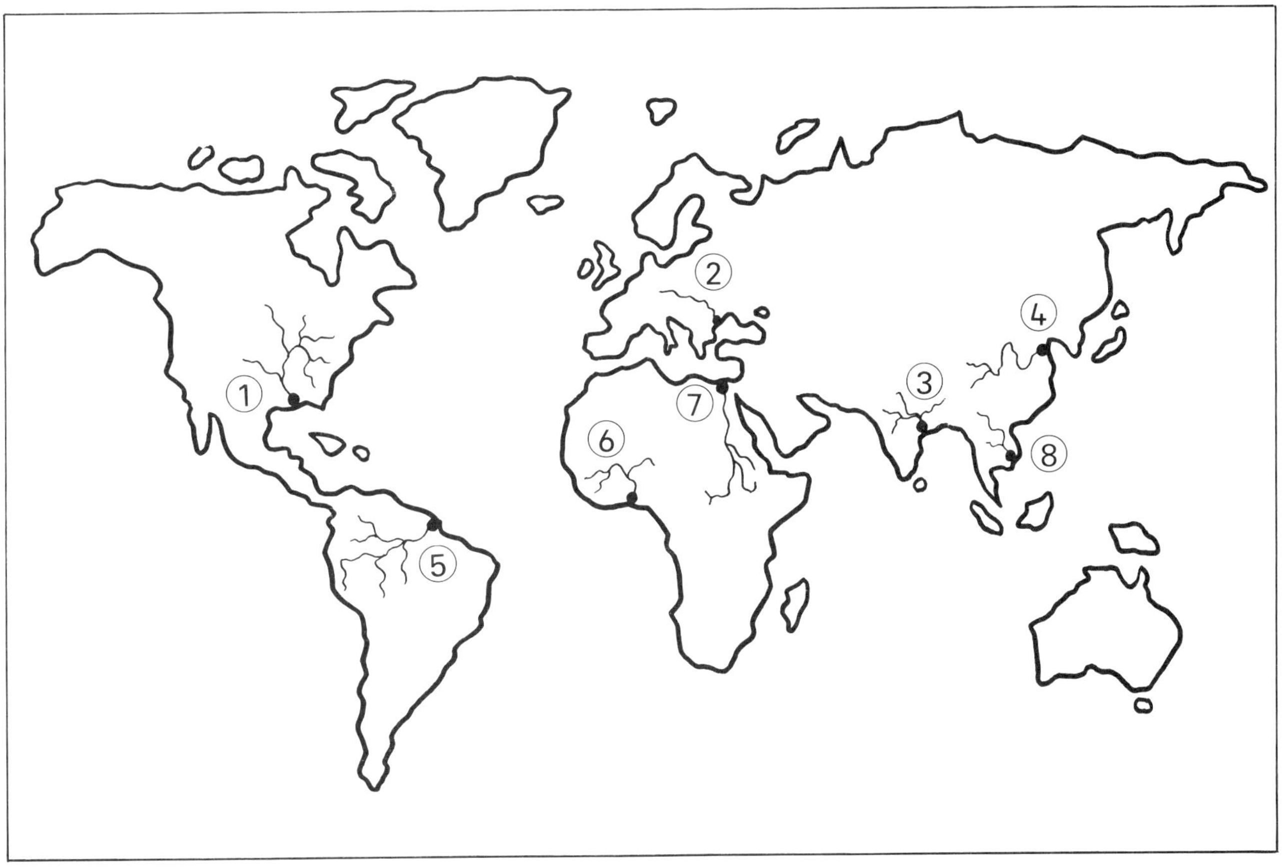

5.	6.	7.	8.

2. Draw a line linking each label to the correct place on the map.

3. Which continent has no important river deltas according to the map?

____

Name ______________________________

Weather conditions

Make drawings for each of the different weather conditions.

Temperature

hot	mild	cool	cold

Wind

calm	gentle breeze	strong breeze	gale

Cloud

clear sky	sunny spells	showers	rain

Name ______________________________

Sun and shade

1. In the table below, make a list of surfaces and materials found in your school grounds.
2. Record the sun and shade temperature for each material, using an electric thermometer.

Material	Sun temperature	Shade temperature

3. Which material gets hottest in the sun? ______________________________

   Can you think why? ______________________________

   Which material stays coldest? ______________________________

   Can you think why? ______________________________

Name ______________________________

Different sites

1. Visit four different sites around your school.
2. Think about each place in turn. Circle or colour the word in each column that best describes the temperature, wind and surface.

Place ____________________

Temperature	Wind	Surface
cold (below 10 °C)	still	dry
average (10–20 °C)	gentle breeze	damp to touch
hot (over 20 °C)	very windy	lying water

Place ____________________

Temperature	Wind	Surface
cold (below 10 °C)	still	dry
average (10–20 °C)	gentle breeze	damp to touch
hot (over 20 °C)	very windy	lying water

Place ____________________

Temperature	Wind	Surface
cold (below 10 °C)	still	dry
average (10–20 °C)	gentle breeze	damp to touch
hot (over 20 °C)	very windy	lying water

Place ____________________

Temperature	Wind	Surface
cold (below 10 °C)	still	dry
average (10–20 °C)	gentle breeze	damp to touch
hot (over 20 °C)	very windy	lying water

3. When did you make your survey?

Date ____________________ Time ____________________

Name ______________________________

Site conditions

1. Find out what the children of Darwin Primary School discovered when they made a survey of site conditions. Add up the ticks in the table to work out the total for each place around the school.

2. Colour the circle that matches the score. Use red for two or more ticks and blue for one tick or less.

Place	Surface	Conditions: Sunny?	Dry?	Sheltered?	Number of ticks	Warm and dry 2 ticks or more	Chilly and damp 1 tick or less
playground	tarmac	✓	✓	✗		○	○
car park	concrete	✗	✓	✓		○	○
alleyway	brick	✗	✗	✗		○	○
field	grass	✓	✓	✗		○	○
pond	water	✗	✗	✓		○	○
trees	leaves	✗	✗	✓		○	○
garden	earth	✓	✓	✓		○	○

3. Colour the circles on the plan to show these results.

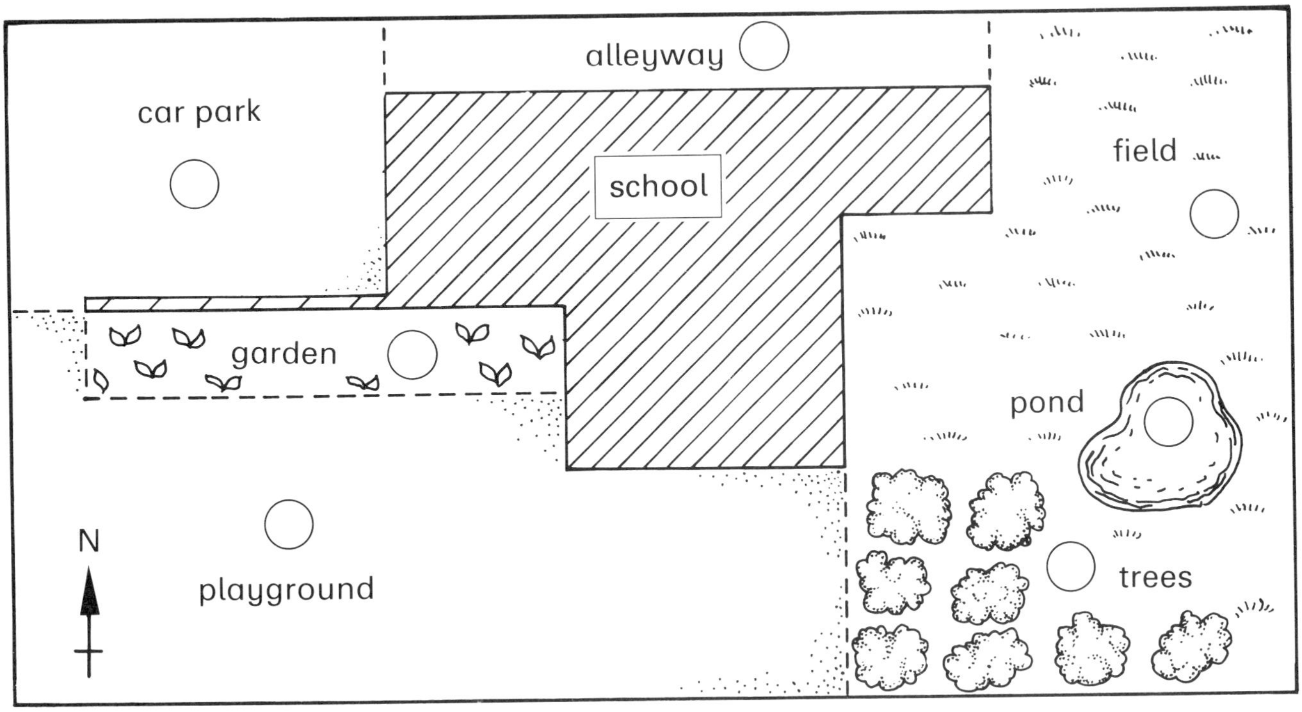

Name ______________________________

London climate graph

1. The table below shows average monthly temperatures and rainfall for London. Show these figures on the empty graphs. Use a line for temperature and blocks for rainfall.

	Winter			Spring			Summer			Autumn		
	D	J	F	M	A	M	J	J	A	S	O	N
Temperature °C	7	6	7	10	13	17	20	22	21	19	14	10
Rainfall mm	50	55	40	35	40	45	45	55	60	50	55	65

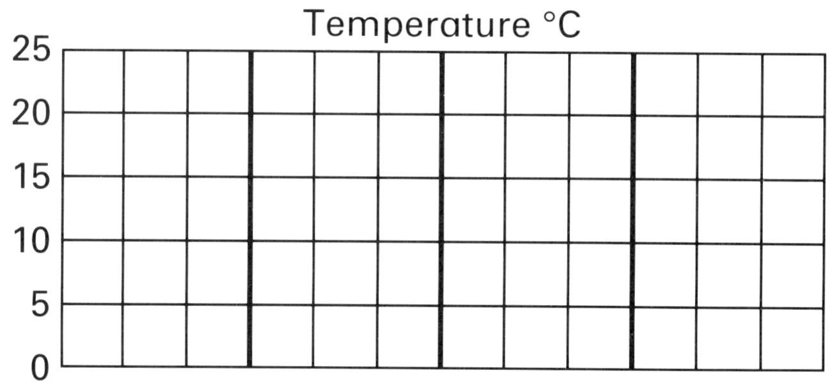

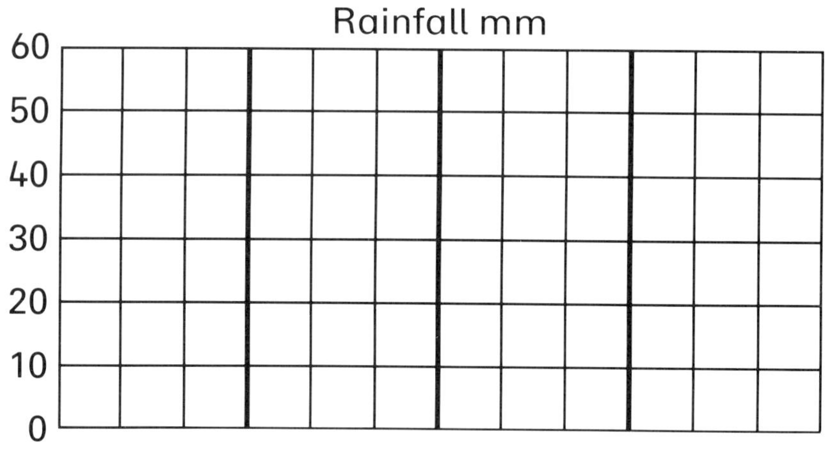

2. Use the information from the graphs to help you describe each season.

	Winter	Spring	Summer	Autumn
Temperature				
Rainfall				

Name ______________________________

The farmer's year

1. Write down the name of a farm you have studied.
   (a) Name of farm ....
   (b) UK county or region ....

2. Write down the jobs done each season on the dial below.

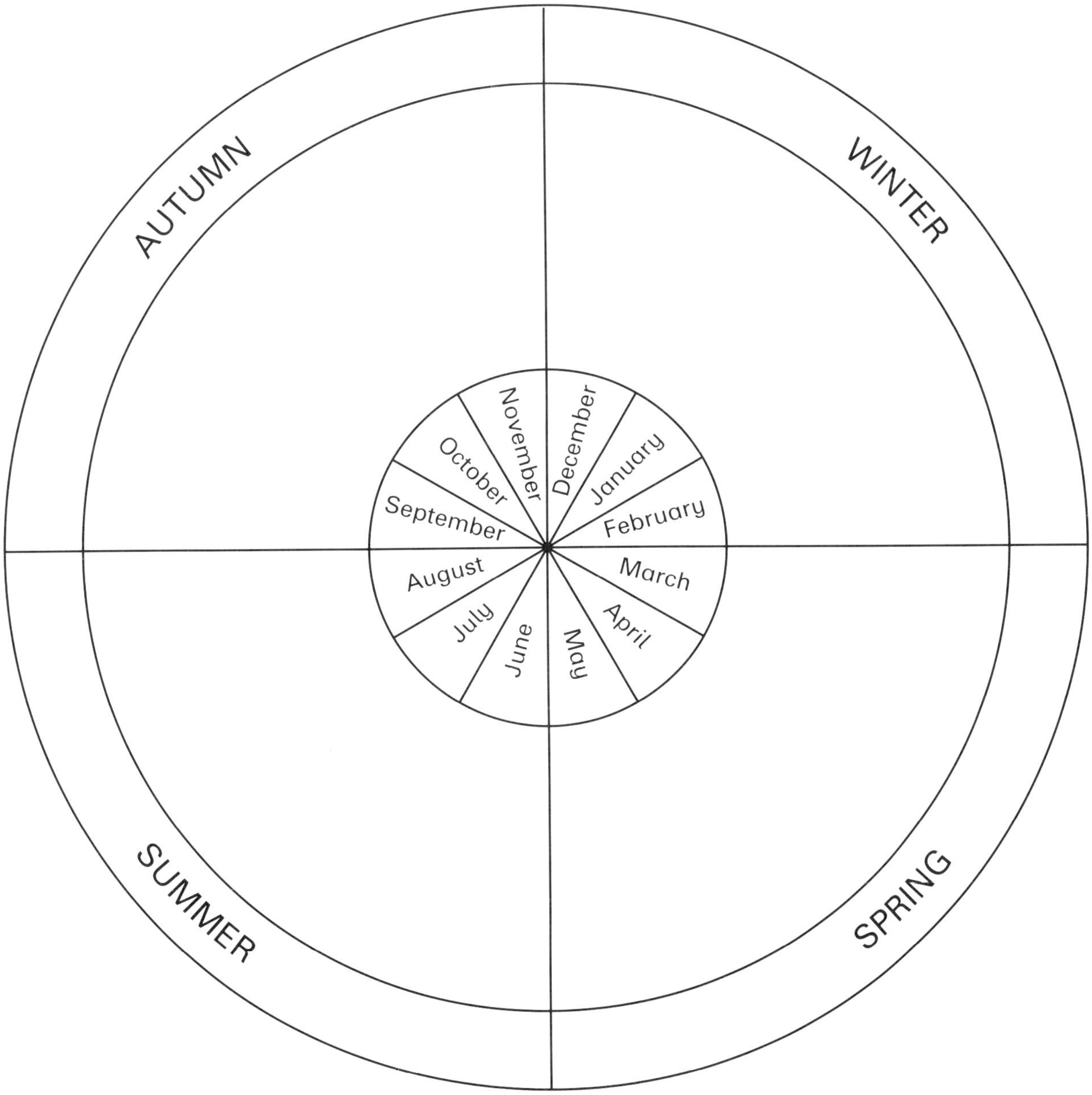

Name ______________________

Summer and winter

1. Colour the pictures
2. Write a sentence explaining what they show.

June each year

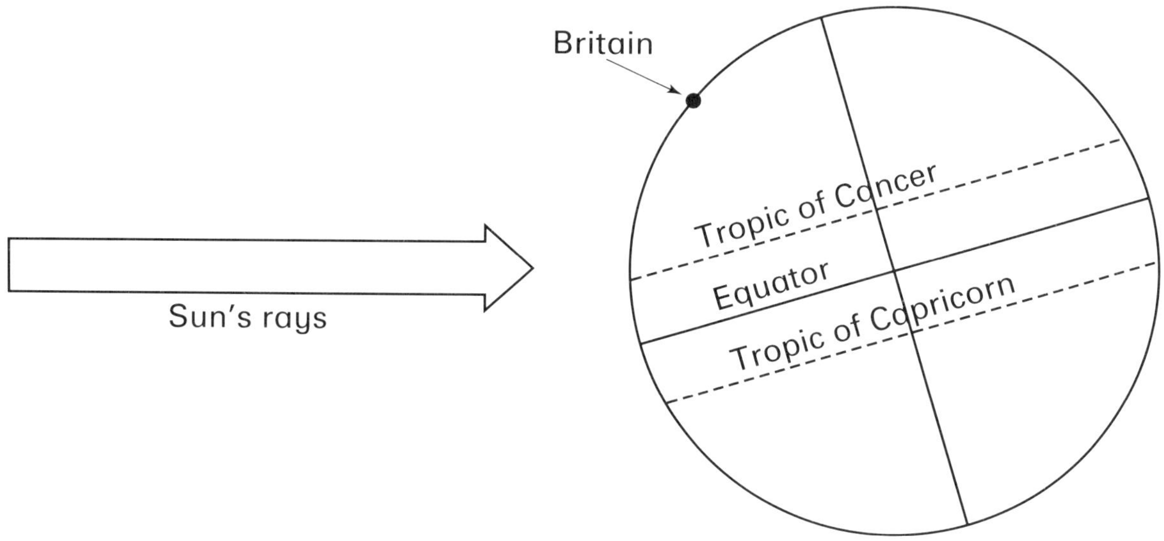

December each year

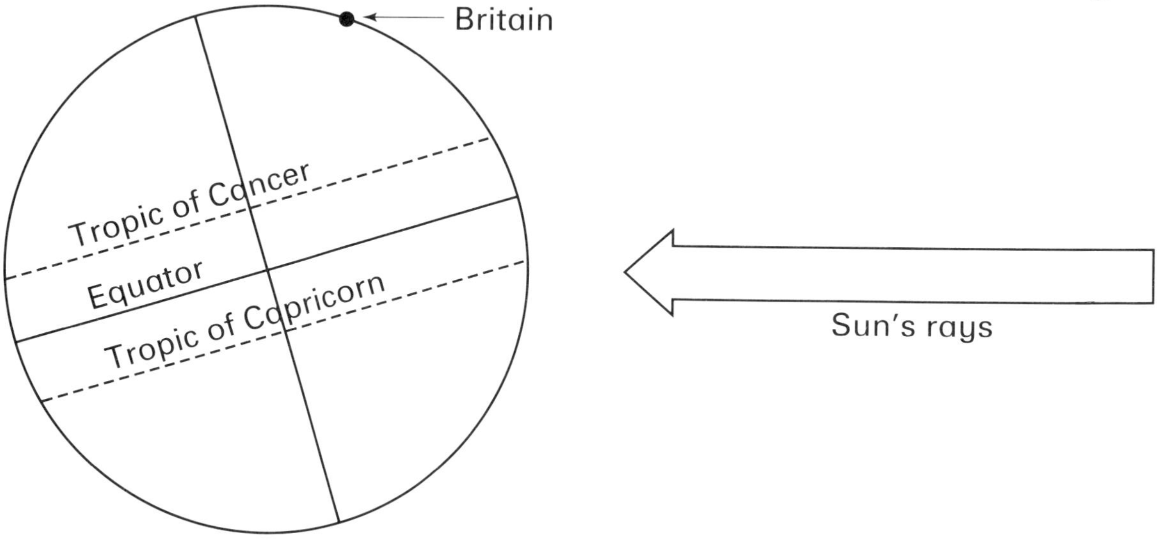

Name ______________________________

Weather worldwide

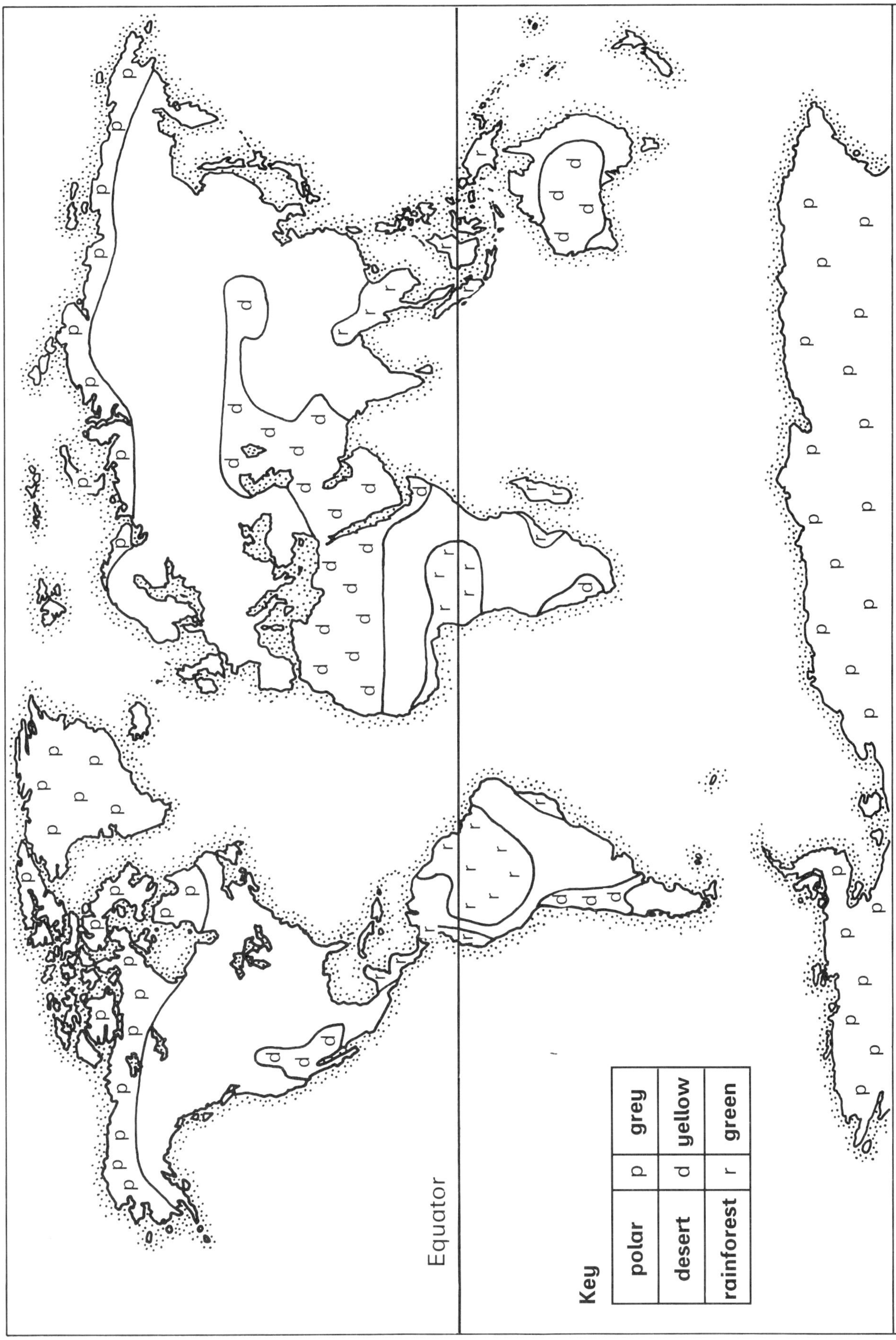

Key

polar	p	grey
desert	d	yellow
rainforest	r	green

1. Colour the code boxes in the Key.
2. Colour the world map using this code.

Name ______________________________

Contrasts

1. Colour the pictures.
2. Circle the words that best describe the temperature and rainfall in each place.

Polar regions
It is very cold and dry here. There is snow even in summer and icebergs float in the sea.

Temperature	Rainfall
hot	wet
cold	dry

Desert regions
Deserts are usually hot and dry. It rains so little that very few plants can grow.

Temperature	Rainfall
hot	wet
cold	dry

Rainforests
Rainforests are hot, steamy and wet. The trees and plants grow quickly.

Temperature	Rainfall
hot	wet
cold	dry

Name ______________________________

Rainforest products

Name the different rainforest products using the list below.

sugar   chickens   bananas   medicines   pineapples

car tyres   railway sleepers   chewing gum

b _ _ _ _ _ _

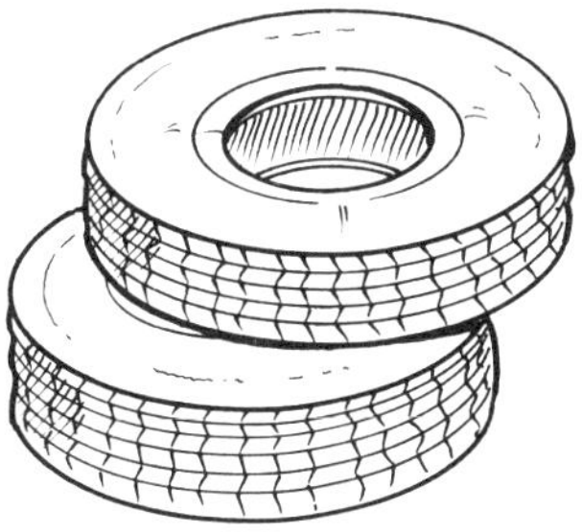

c _ _   t _ _ _ _

s _ _ _ _

m _ _ _ _ _ _ _ _

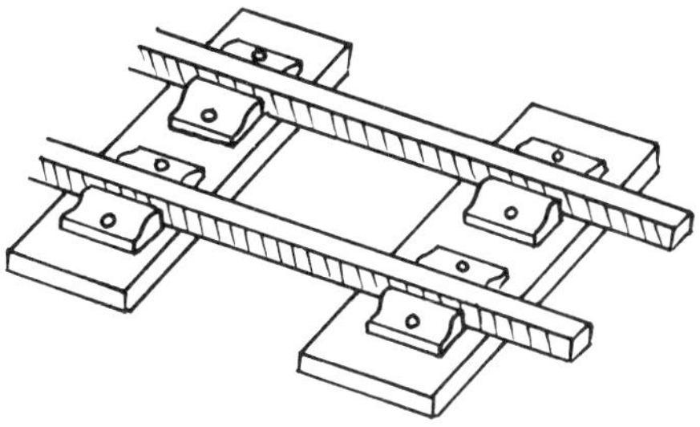

r _ _ _ _ _ _

s _ _ _ _ _ _ _

c _ _ _ _ _ _

g _ _

p _ _ _ _ _ _ _ _ _

c _ _ _ _ _ _ _

Name ______________________________

House plants

1. Colour the pictures of the plants.

rubber plant 	cactus 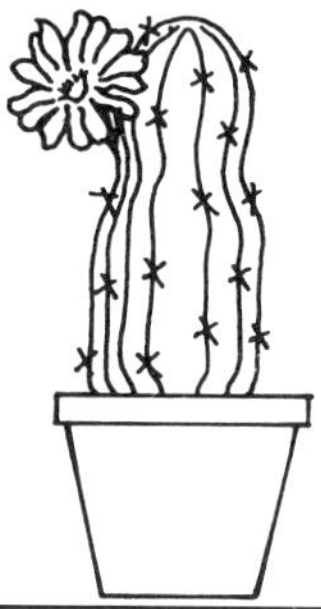	stonecrop 
Equatorial Likes hot, wet conditions.	**Desert** Likes hot, dry conditions.	**Polar** Likes cold, dry conditions.

2. Decide which room of the house would suit each plant best then complete the table below.

Room	Conditions	Climate	Plant
porch	cold and dry		
living room	hot and dry		
bathroom	hot and wet		

3. Draw the plants on the picture of the house.

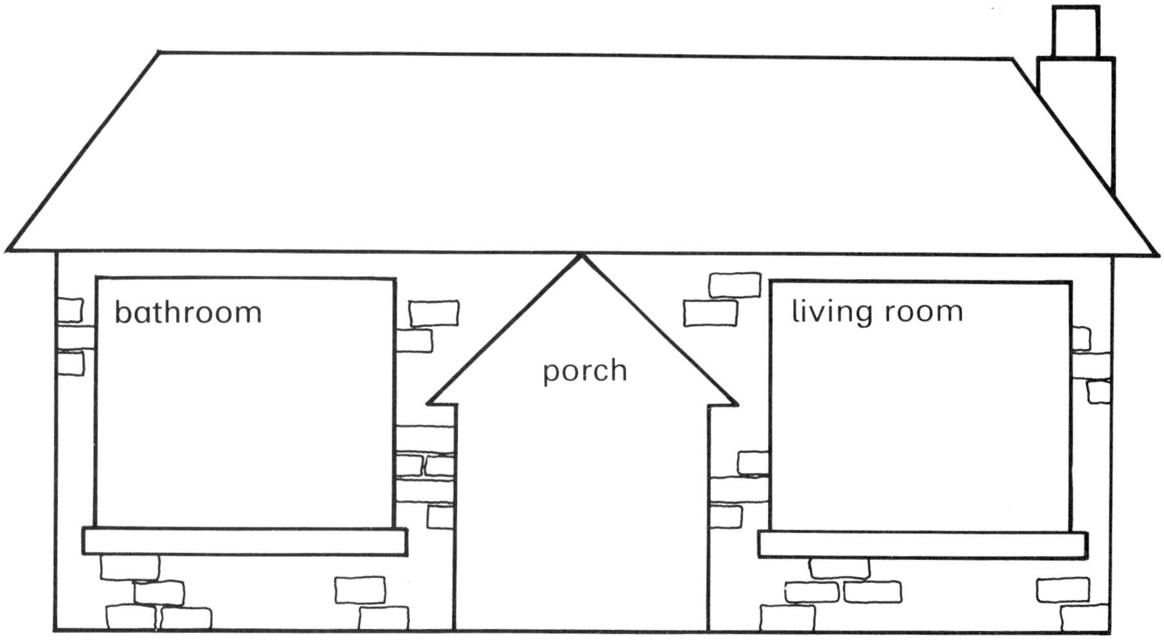

Name ______________________________

Types of town

1. Colour the pictures.
2. Write each label under the correct picture.

Strong point	Crossing point	Market town
Industrial town	Port	Resort

1. Castle

2. Old bridge

3. Animal market

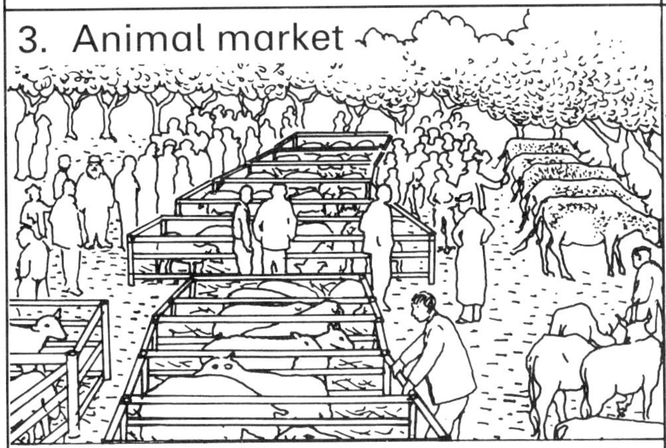

4. Large factory

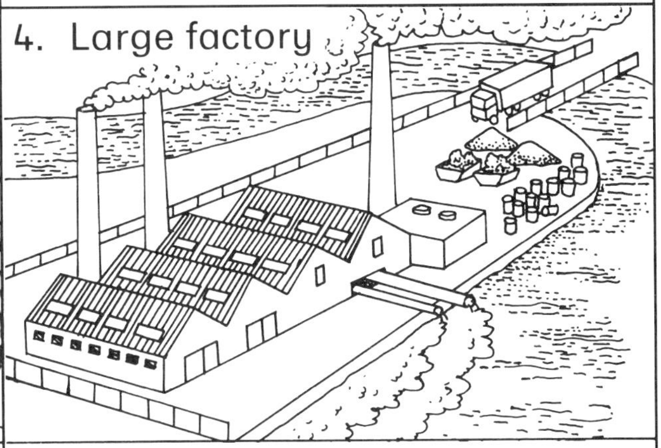

5. Harbour

6. Beach

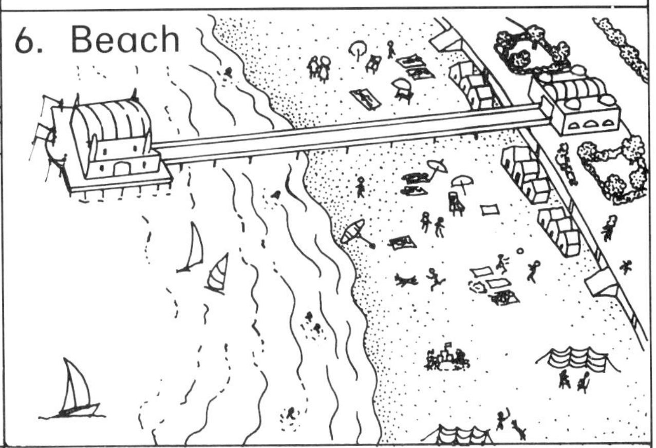

Name ______________________________

Historic towns

1. Working from a map of Roman Britain, make a list of Roman towns on the table below.
2. Which of these towns is nearest to the place where you live?

____

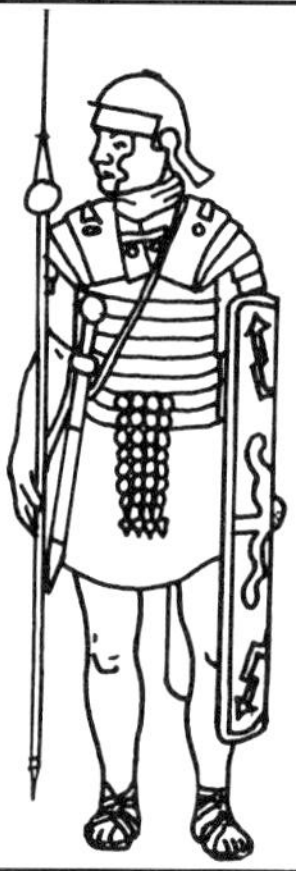

Roman name	Modern name

Name ______________________________

City search

1. Circle the twelve cities on the word search, reading either down or across.

N	A	E	D	I	N	B	U	R	G	H	B	G	J
E	C	G	O	D	F	I	I	H	L	A	E	S	G
W	I	E	B	B	E	R	C	T	A	S	U	H	I
C	S	M	E	R	A	M	D	S	S	B	A	B	M
A	T	F	L	I	E	I	D	I	G	T	D	U	A
S	O	Q	V	S	K	N	S	L	O	N	D	O	N
T	Y	N	B	T	S	G	A	O	W	H	R	W	C
L	R	P	Z	O	S	H	S	A	O	N	A	D	H
E	U	B	E	L	F	A	S	T	Z	P	J	O	E
S	R	H	U	R	T	M	Q	O	L	E	E	D	S
W	R	O	W	E	D	V	I	M	Y	B	H	S	T
X	L	I	V	E	R	P	O	O	L	C	U	K	E
T	E	A	X	C	C	A	R	D	I	F	F	S	R
O	S	O	U	T	H	A	M	P	T	O	N	D	L

2. Name the cities you have discovered.

1.	7.
2.	8.
3.	9.
4.	10.
5.	11.
6.	12.

Name ______________________________

Great cities

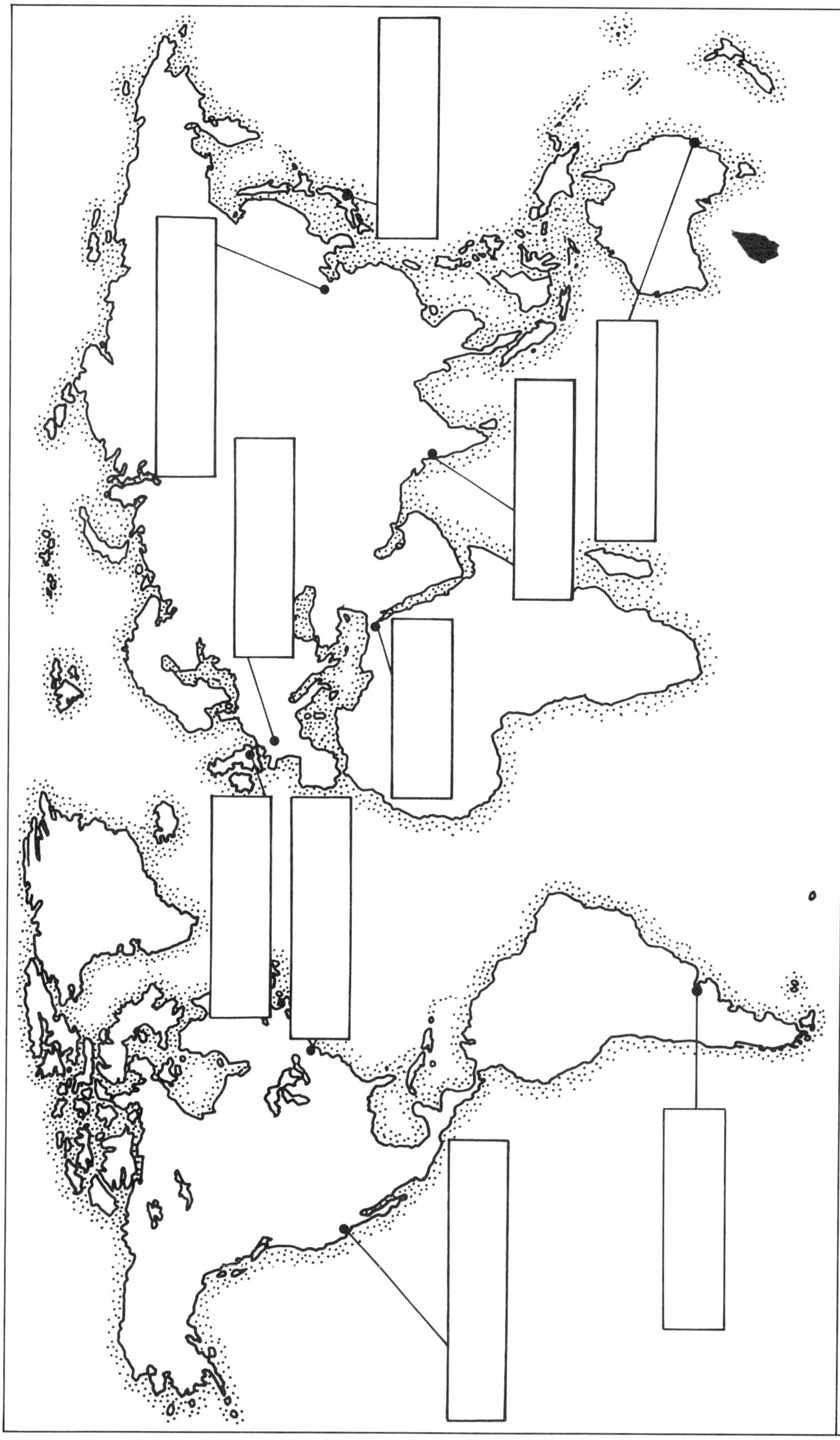

1. Colour the land and sea on the map.
2. Using an atlas, name each city in the empty space.

London	Cairo	Tokyo	Bombay	Buenos Aires
Paris	Beijing	Sydney	New York	Los Angeles

Name ______________________________

Classroom areas

1. Colour the empty boxes next to each symbol. Use a different colour for each one.

study area ☐ art area ☐ computer corner ☐ reading corner ☐

2. Colour the classroom plan using these four colours.

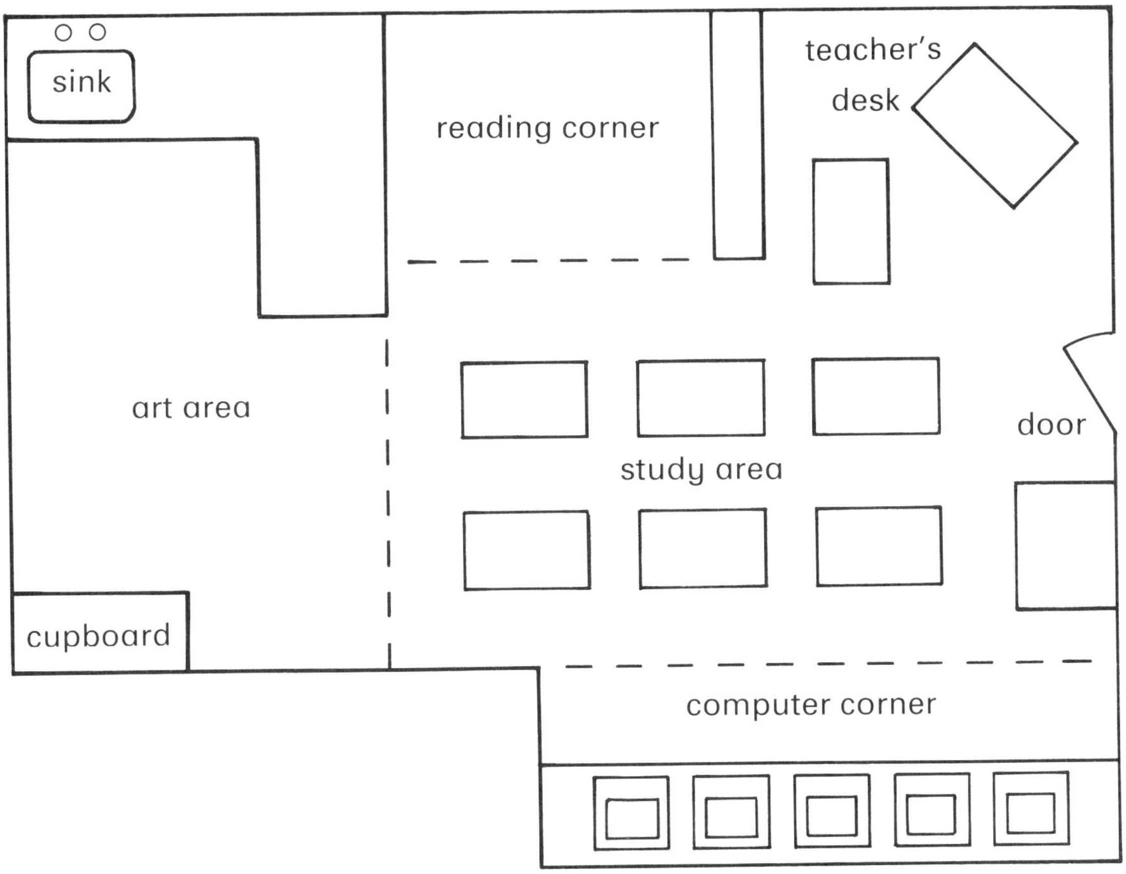

3. Which activity takes up the most space? ______________________

Name ______________________________

School site

1. Colour the code boxes in the table below.

Education		Transport		Leisure	
Red		Blue		Green	
classrooms hall annexe		road car park		playground field garden	

2. Colour the different areas on the plan of Woodside Primary School.

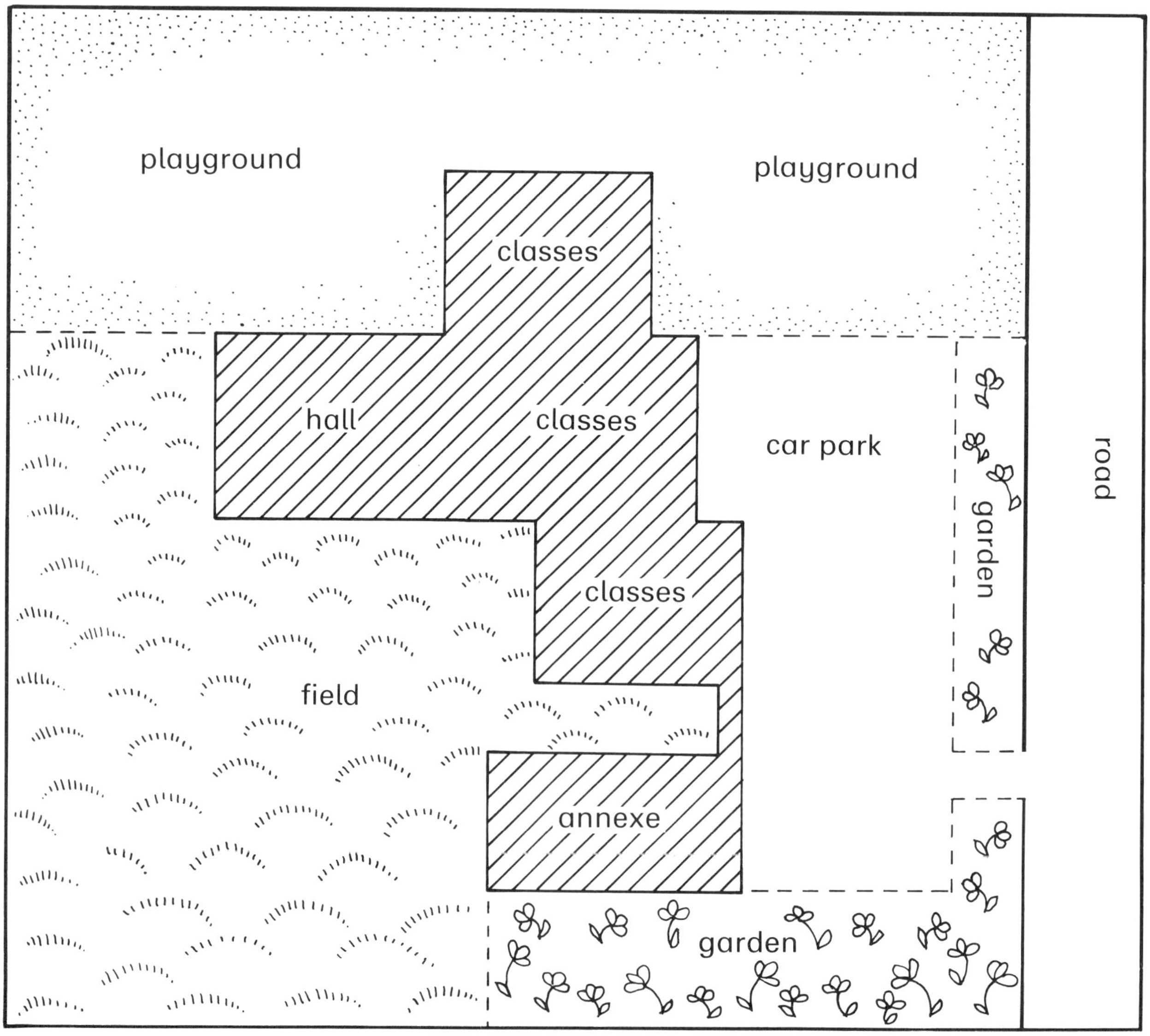

Name ______________________________

Transport survey

1. Visit a street near your school.
2. Make a transport survey over a five-minute period.

Name of street ______________________________

Date ______________________ **Time** ____________

	Tally marks	**Total**
cars 		
lorries 		
vans 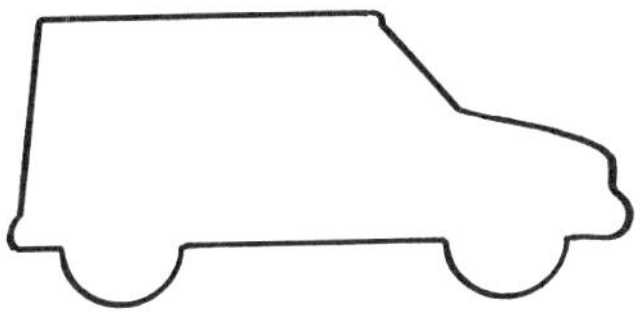		
motorbikes/ pedal bikes 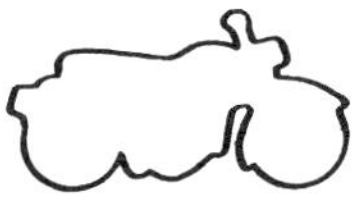		
others		

3. From your survey, what form of transport is used most? ____________

   From your survey, what form of transport is used least? ____________

Name ______________________

Ports and airports

1. Colour land and sea on the map below.
2. Write the names of the ports and airports in the tables.
3. Name the port and airport nearest where you live, and add them to the map if not already shown.

____

____

Ports

Airports

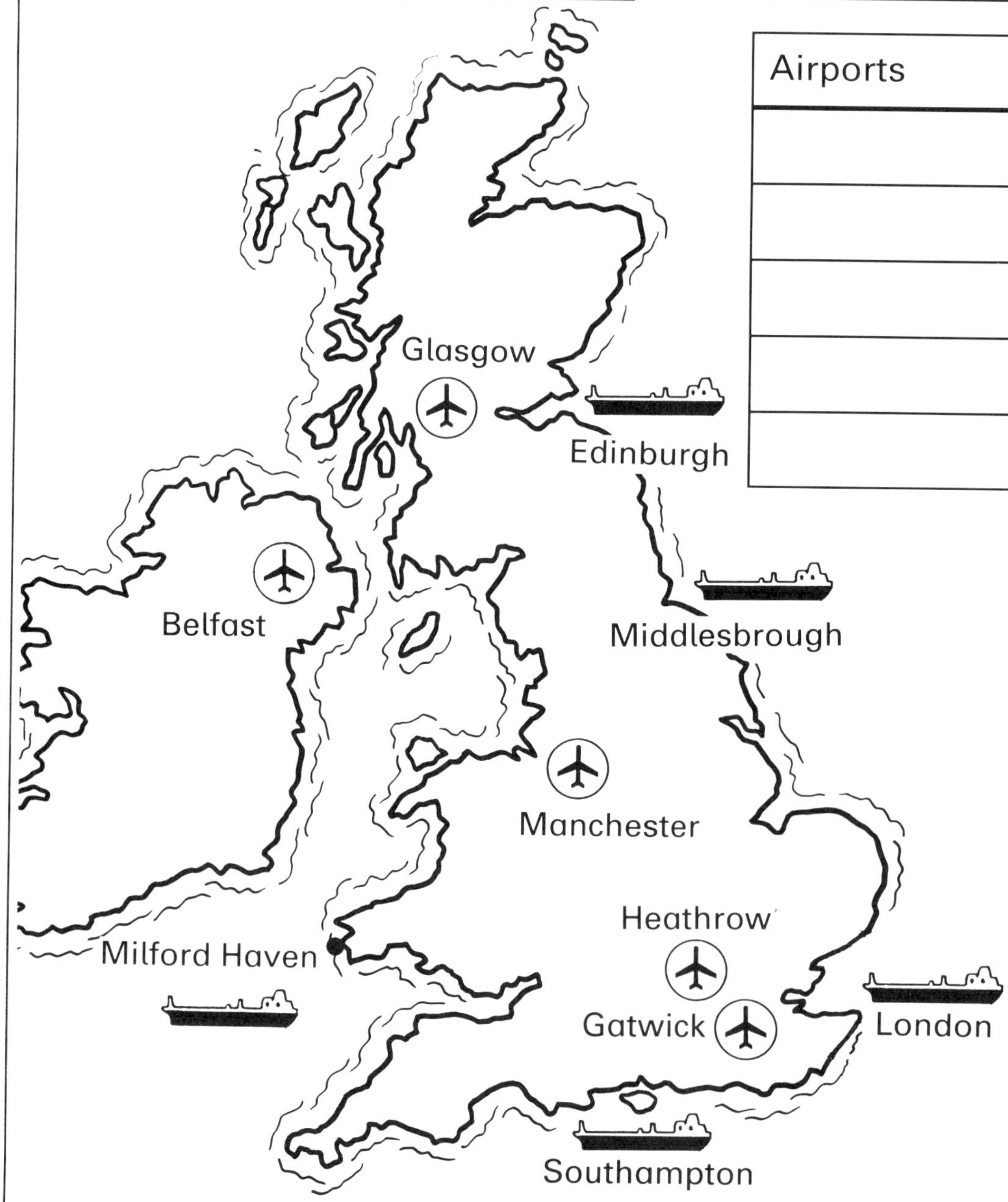

Name ________________________________

Zones

1. Using pictures to help you, do drawings showing different types of land use or zones.
2. Cut out your drawings and pin them to the correct place on a map of your area.

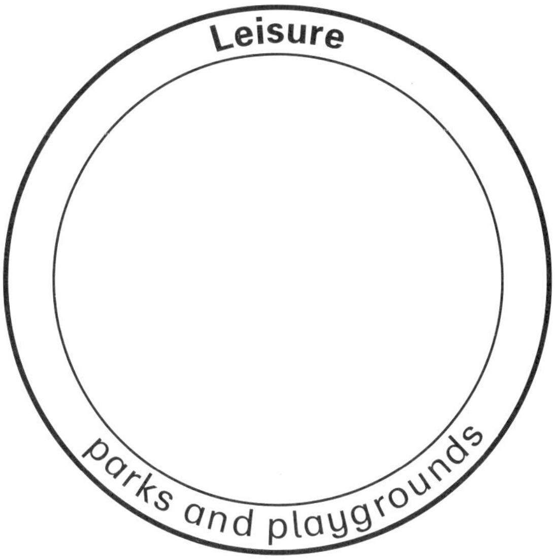

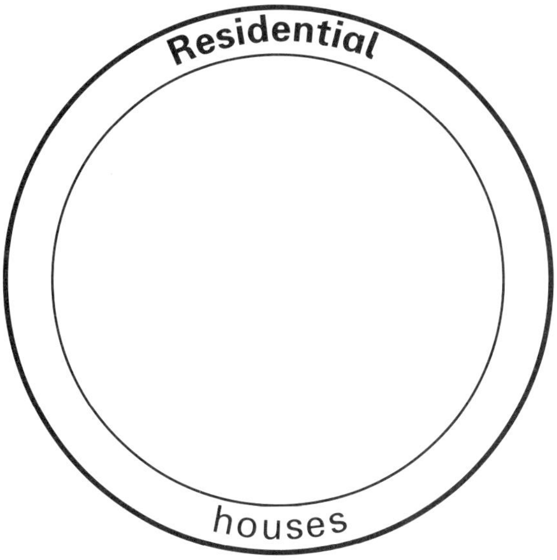

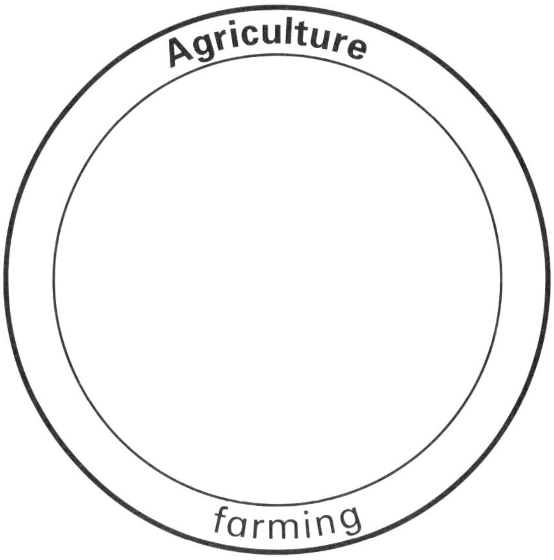

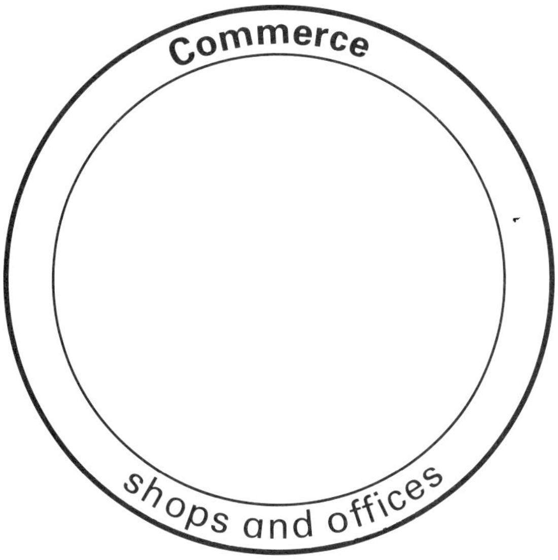

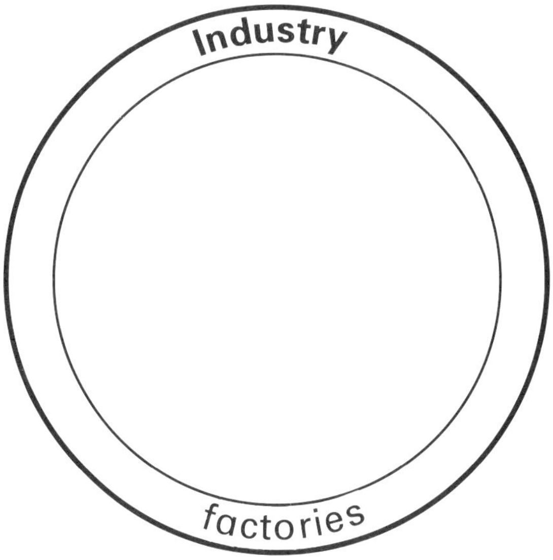

Name ______________________

Factory study

Answer the questions in the spaces below.

What is the factory called?

What does it make?

Where is it situated?

What raw materials does it use?

Where do the raw materials come from?

Where are the goods sent to?

When was it set up here?

What was the reason?

____

____

____

____

____

Name ________________________________

Changes

1. Label the pictures from the list below.

park	houses	bridge	pedestrianisation
school	factory	theatre	sports centre

2. Show the effect of each change by colouring one of the boxes next to the pictures.

	improves services		improves services
	makes movement easier		makes movement easier
	makes a place larger		makes a place larger
	improves services	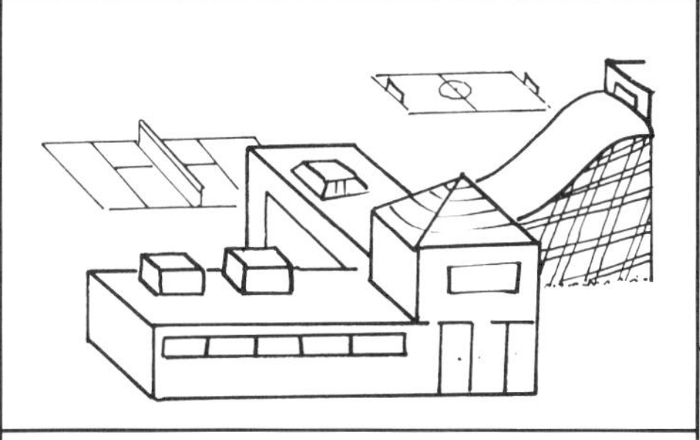	improves services
	makes movement easier		makes movement easier
	makes a place larger		makes a place larger
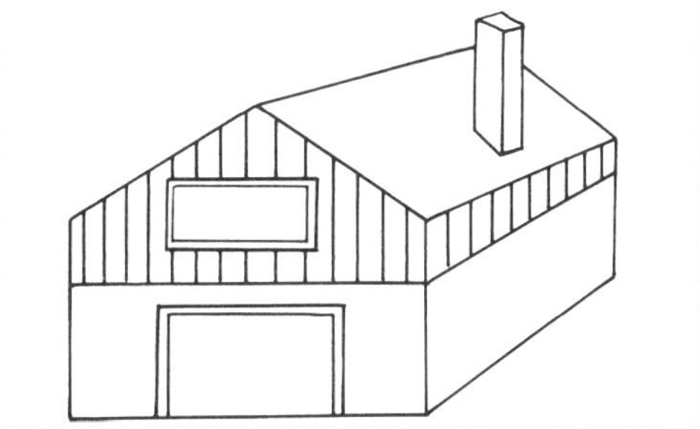	improves services		improves services
	makes movement easier		makes movement easier
	makes a place larger		makes a place larger
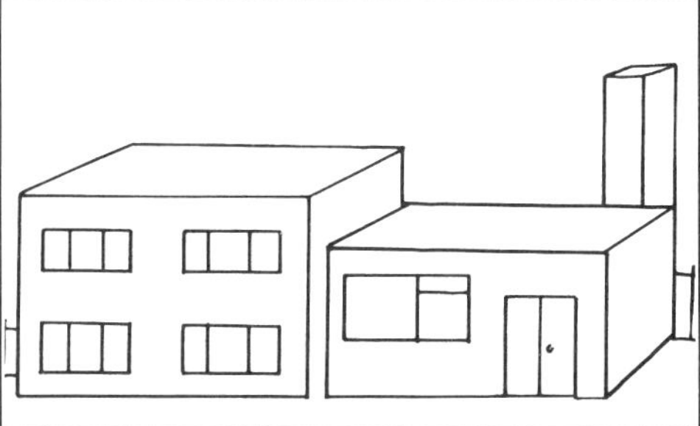	improves services	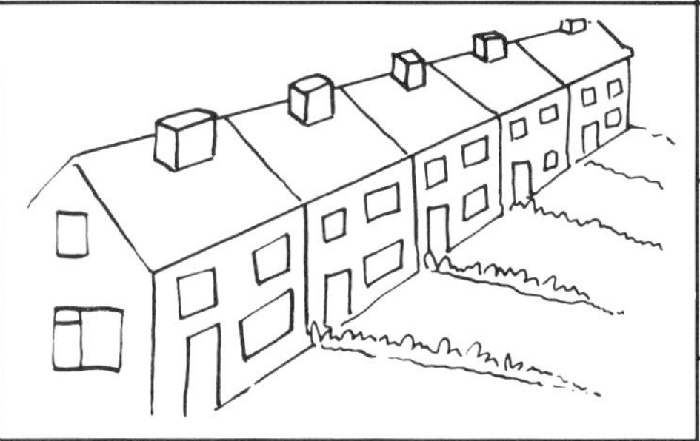	improves services
	makes movement easier		makes movement easier
	makes a place larger		makes a place larger

Name ______________________________

Suitable sites

1. Think about the developments listed in the table. Tick the site conditions you think are important in deciding where to place each development.

Development	Site conditions: rich fertile soil	flat land	sand and gravel	close to railway	away from houses	close to motorway	in the hills
quarry							
farm							
airport							
large factory							
race-track							
nature reserve							

2. Colour the map below.

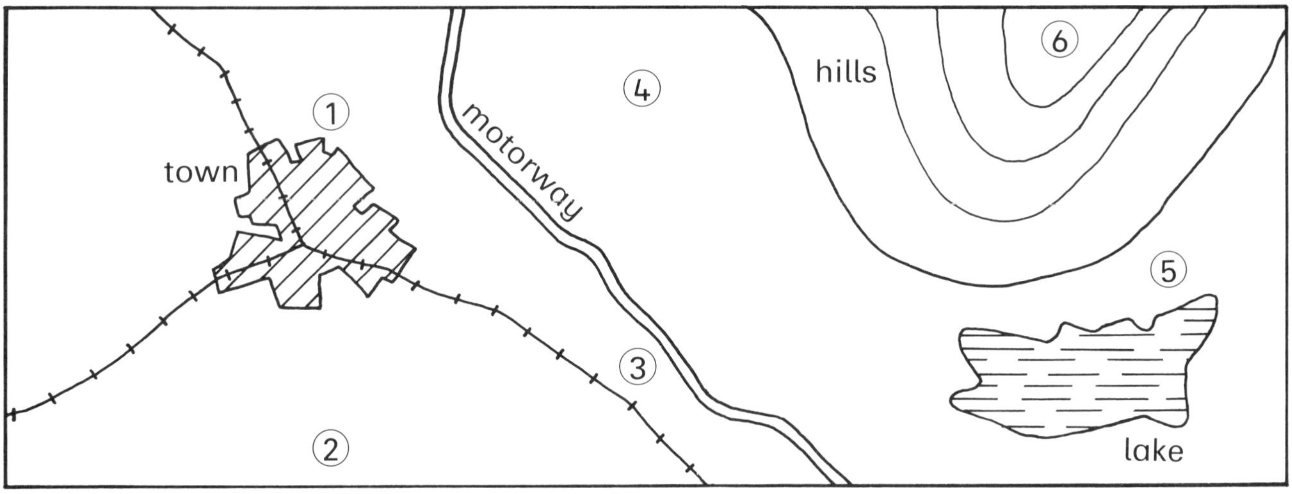

3. Look at the sites marked with a number. Decide which one you would choose for a) a large factory, and b) a motor racing track.

4. Complete the sentences below.

I choose site ◯ for the large factory because ______________________________

____

I choose site ◯ for the race track because ______________________________

____

Name ________________________________

New facilities

1. Ask sixteen people what new facilities are needed in your area. Get them to choose one of the things in the table and put a tick to show their answer.

	New facilities							
Name of person	playground	ice-skating rink	cinema	car park	sports centre	shops	library	park
Total								

2. Add up the totals.

3. What facility seems most needed? ________________________

Name ________________________________

New motorway

1. Read what the different people think about the plan to build a new motorway and colour the pictures.

Joan Adams
receptionist

I am fed up with all the traffic jams. The motorway will help me get to work.

John Driver
old age pensioner

The motorway will cost a lot of money. I cannot afford more taxes.

George Smith
farmer

The motorway will cut my farm in two and spoil the peace of the countryside.

Lucy Harris
conservationist

The motorway will destroy many valuable plants and creatures.

Jack Green
shopkeeper

Lots of people will get jobs building the motorway which will help the unemployed.

Penny Jones
councillor

We need the motorway to take the traffic away from our town.

Peter Davis
lorry driver

The motorway will help me to deliver goods quickly.

Richard Page
teacher

The motorway will not solve the traffic problem. It will just create pollution.

Elizabeth Potter
planner

We have looked at all the possibilities and the motorway is the best solution.

2. Make a list of the people on a separate piece of paper. Say if they are for or against the motorway and give their reasons.

Name ________________________

Severn barrage

There is a scheme to build a barrage across the River Severn. This would make electricity by harnessing the power of the tide.

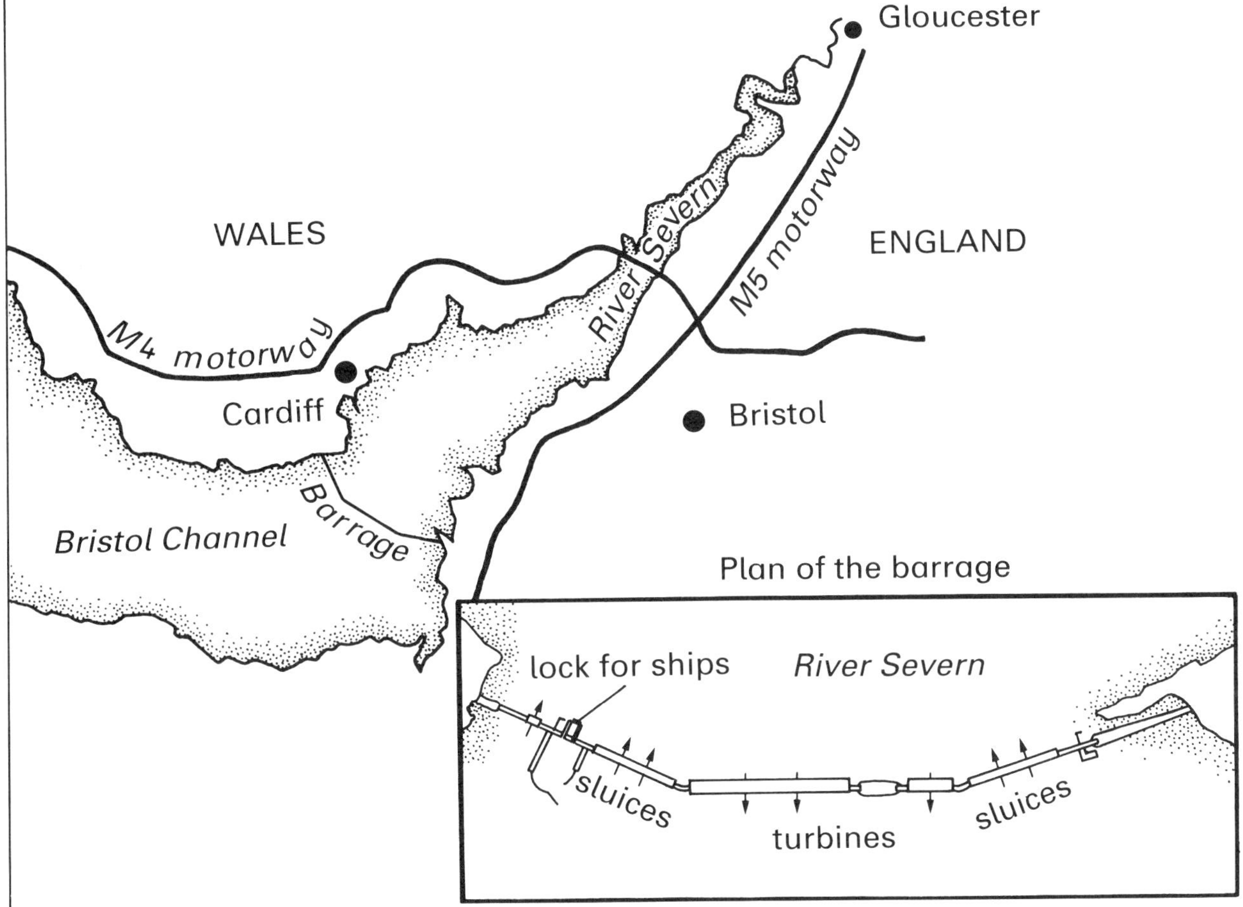

Key facts

- The barrage could generate about 7% of the electricity we use in England and Wales.
- The Severn is a good site because the river estuary funnels the site.
- The barrage could seriously affect birds that live on the mud flats.
- There would be a main road across the top of the barrage.
- The scheme would create about 20 000 permanent jobs in local industry and tourism.
- The barrage would make electricity without causing pollution.
- The barrage would be very expensive to build.
- The peace and quiet of nearby country areas would be lost.

Name ______________________________

Channel Tunnel

The Channel Tunnel opened in 1994. For the first time in history, there is a land route between England and France, with a frequent shuttle service of fast trains linking the two countries.

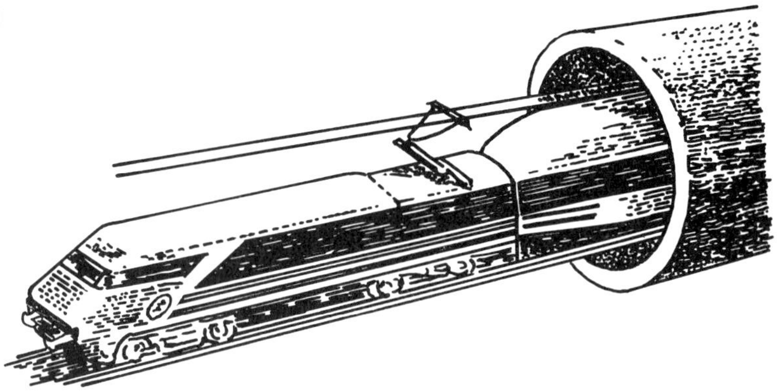

Arguments in favour of the Tunnel		
Trade	Travel	Industry
	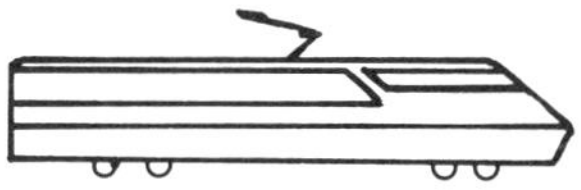	
The Tunnel is vital to trade. It is estimated that freight traffic will double within twenty years of its opening.	It will be much quicker to travel once the Tunnel has opened. The journey time from London to Paris will be cut from 6 to 3 hours.	Factories in the Midlands, northern England and Scotland will be 'closer' to mainland Europe, and therefore much better able to compete for markets.

Arguments against the Tunnel		
Jobs	Environment	Safety

Many people who currently work on the ferries will be put out of a job. At least 10 000 jobs could be lost.	The Tunnel will spoil a large area of beautiful countryside and lead to new roads in many parts of south-east England.	The Tunnel may create many new dangers. People say Tunnel fires would be hard to control, terrorists could plant bombs, and rabies could spread to England.

Name ________________________________

Narmada Dams – India

The dams which are planned for the Narmada River in India are some of the largest in the world.

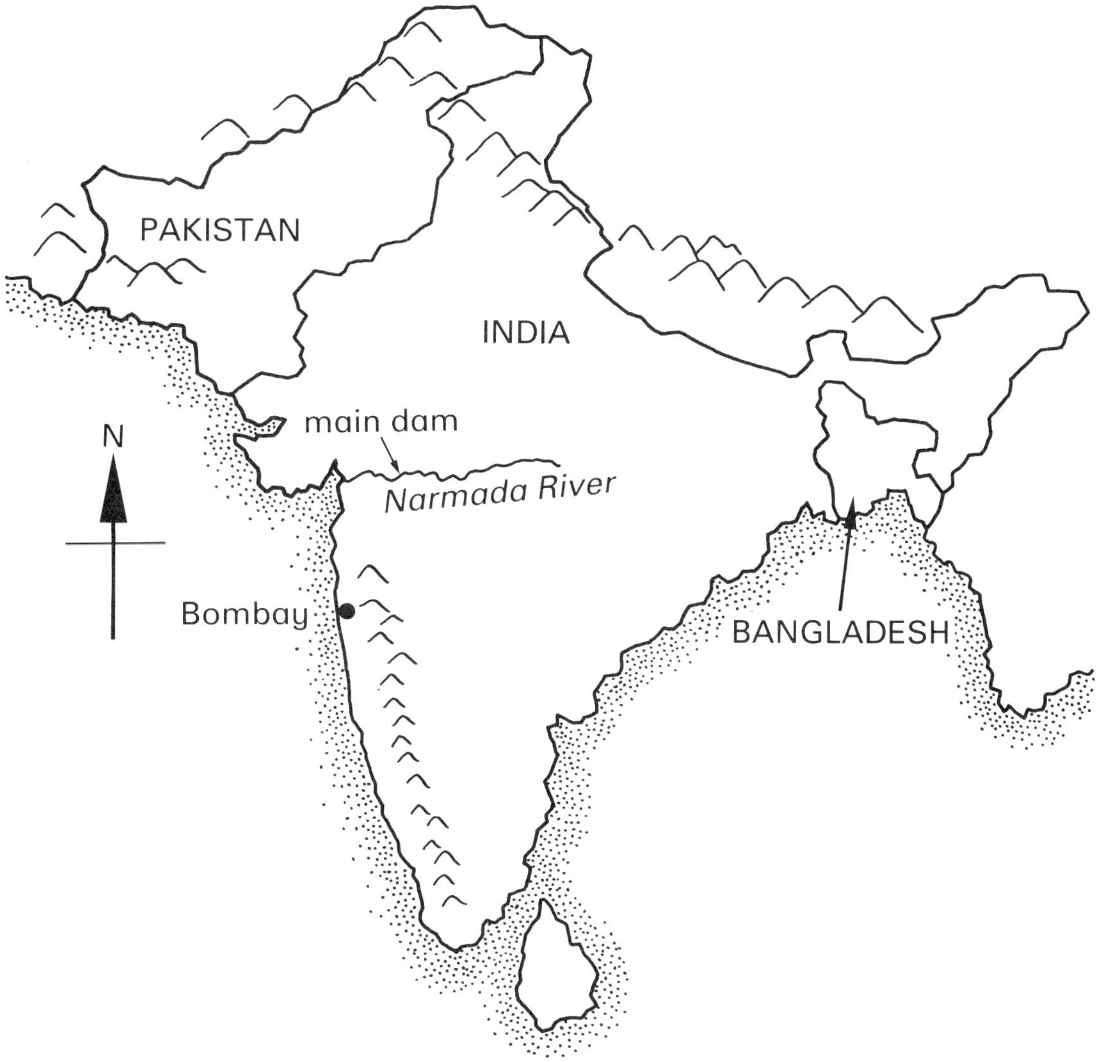

Arguments against the dams

- Rare wildlife and historic sites will be destroyed.
- Fertile farmland and forests will be flooded.
- 200 000 people will be driven from their homes.
- The lake will spread new diseases.
- Poor people will not benefit.

Arguments in favour of the dams

- The scheme will generate electricity.
- It will provide water to help farmers grow crops.
- It will bring drinking water to thousands of villages.
- Fish will be able to live on the lake providing food.
- It will bring money and jobs to a poor area.

Name ________________________________

Carajas Project – Brazil

In 1980, engine trouble forced a helicopter to land on the Carajas Mountains in the rainforests of Brazil. It was carrying a surveyor. He discovered the largest and richest deposits of iron-ore in the world.

Between 1982 and 1987 the Brazilian government set up a huge iron-ore mine. It involved a special railway running 900 kilometres through the forest to Sao Luis on the coast.

Now smelters are being built around the mine. These consume vast amounts of wood each year. Cattle ranches are also being set up. Not only is the forest being destroyed, the Indians who used to live there are being driven out.

The Carajas Project covers a huge area of Brazil. People are worried that before long most of the rainforest will have disappeared.

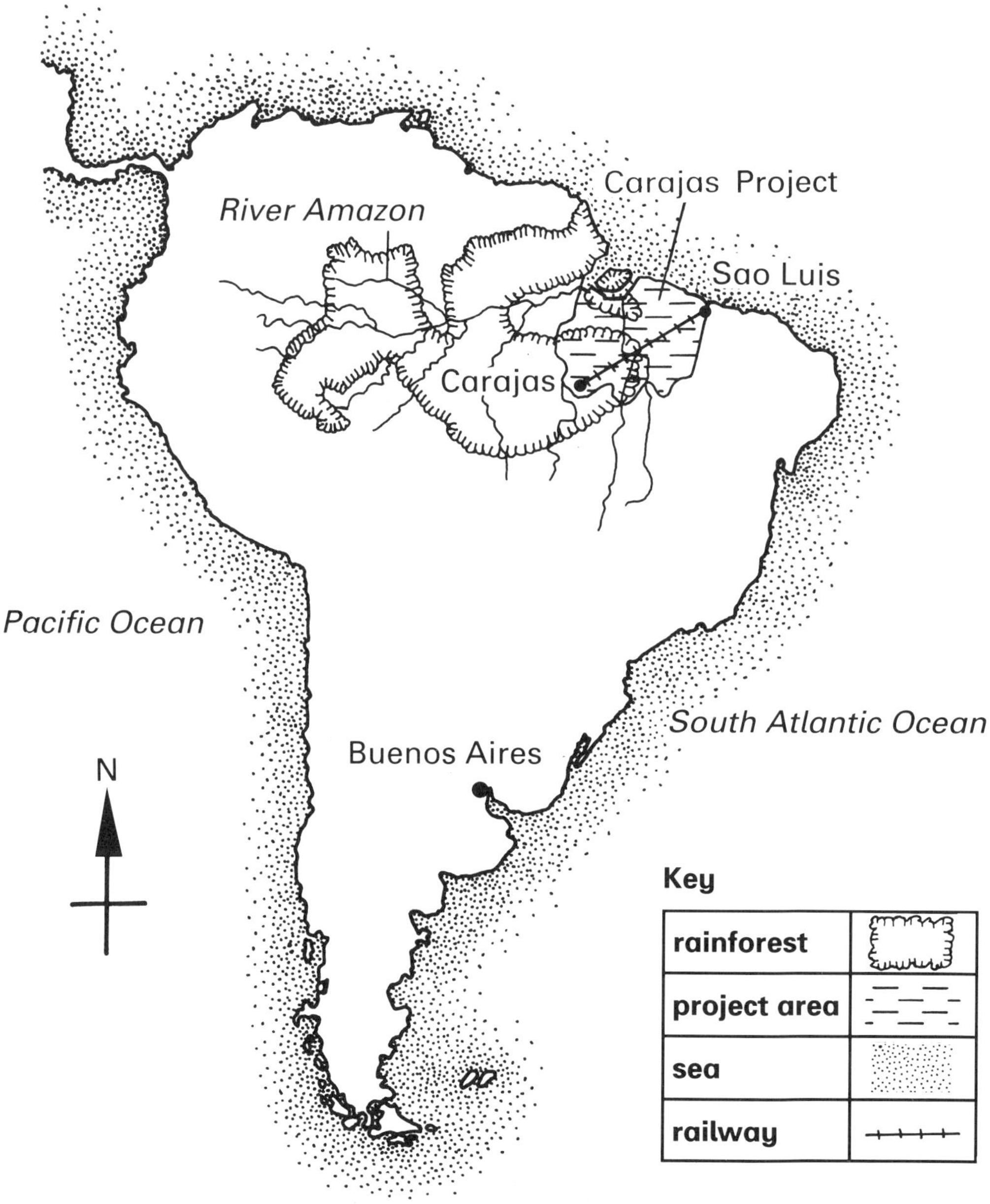

Name ______________________________

Street survey

1. Write down the name of the street and the date of your survey in the empty spaces.

street

[ ]

date

[ ]

2. Colour the circle between each pair of words which best describes your opinion. Colour the centre circle if your feelings are neutral.

noisy	○	○	○	quiet
smelly	○	○	○	fresh
trees	○	○	○	no trees
colourful	○	○	○	drab
tidy	○	○	○	untidy
ugly	○	○	○	beautiful
dark	○	○	○	light
boring	○	○	○	interesting
open	○	○	○	shut in
like	○	○	○	dislike

Name ______________________________

Pollution problems

1. Make a list of ten pollution problems in the area round your school.
2. Decide how long you think each will last and colour the correct box to show your answer.

	How long will it last?		
Pollution problem	under 1 year	1–10 years	over 10 years
1.			
2.			
3.			
4.			
5.			
6.			
7.			
8.			
9.			
10.			

3. Say how one of the problems could be solved?

____

____

____

____

____

Name ______________________________

Derelict land

Working from the picture, make a list in the table below of the way the land has been damaged.

1.	6.
2.	7.
3.	8.
4.	9.
5.	10.

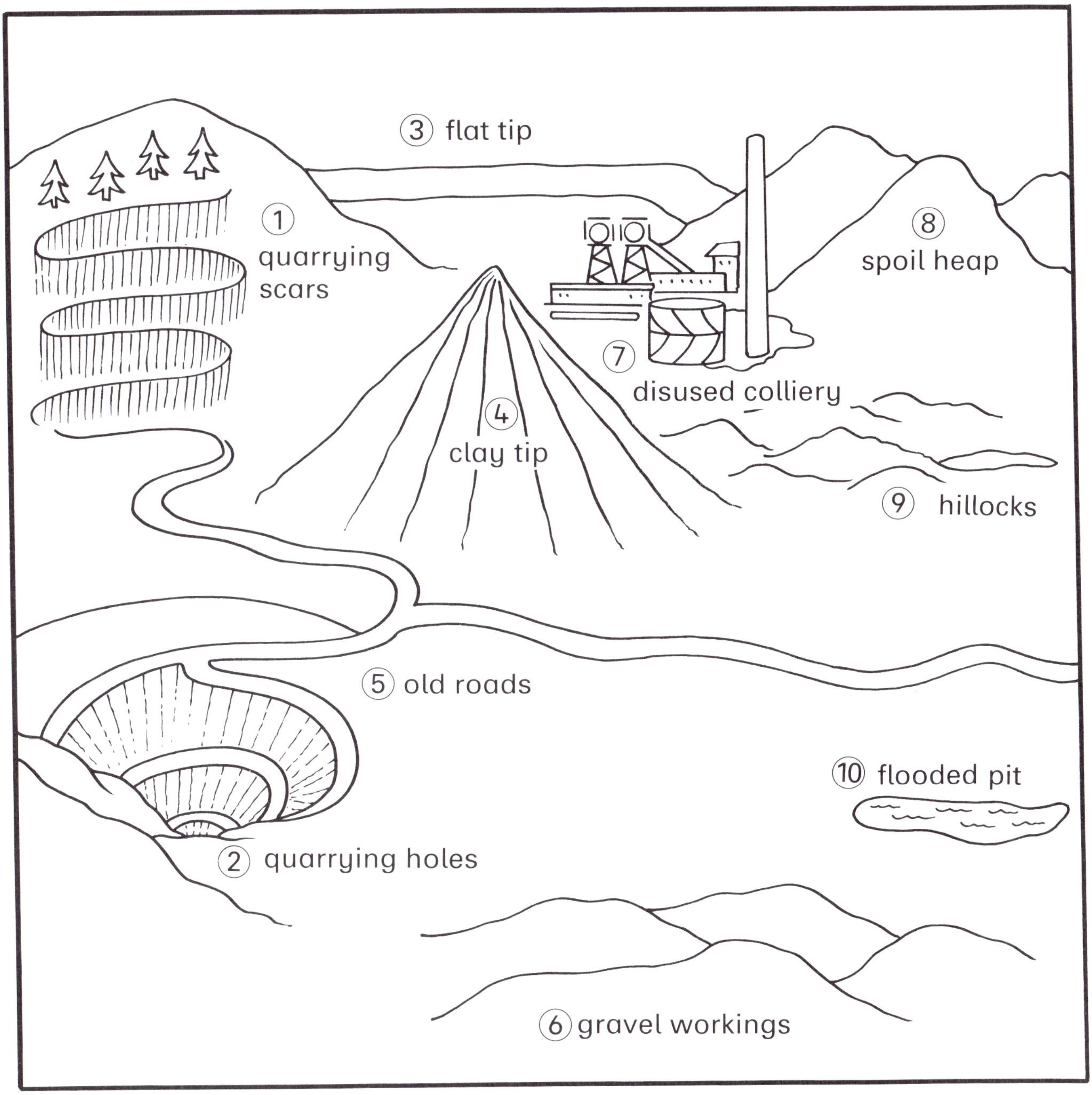

Name ______________________________

Quarry schemes

1. Read the table below to discover eight new uses for an old quarry.

New uses for quarry	Comments
rubbish dump	Unpleasant for local people.
small factory	Could be hidden from view.
nature reserve	A good habitat for plants and creatures.
motor cycle racing	Would provide facility for local youngsters, but noisy.
caravan site	Would be used by holiday makers in summer months.
lorry park	Local transport company needs new site.
animal grazing	Nearby farmer wants more space to graze sheep.
clay pigeon shooting	Private club wants to set up in area.

2. Make a list of the new uses in the table below and answer each question with a tick for 'yes' and a cross for 'no'.

3. Add up the total number of ticks.

New uses for quarry	Creates jobs?	Benefits local people?	Benefits people from other areas?	Protects plants and creatures?	Preserves peace and quiet?	Gives people pleasure?	Total

4. Which do you think is most suitable and why?

____

____

Name ______________________________

Water supplies

1. Colour the pictures below.
2. Cut them out and arrange them in a line in the correct order.
3. Glue the pictures down on a separate piece of paper and draw arrows linking them together.

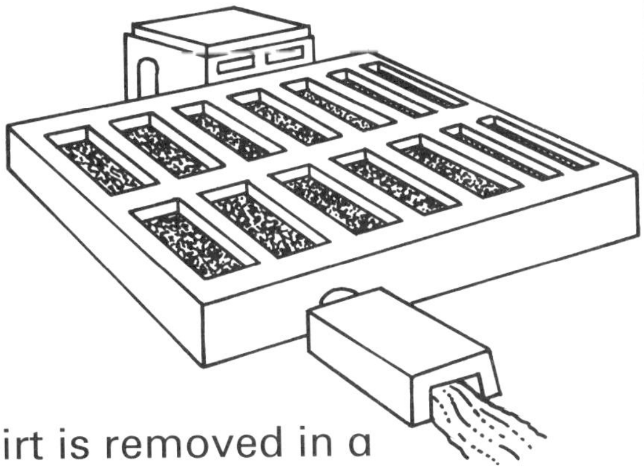

Dirt is removed in a cleaning plant.

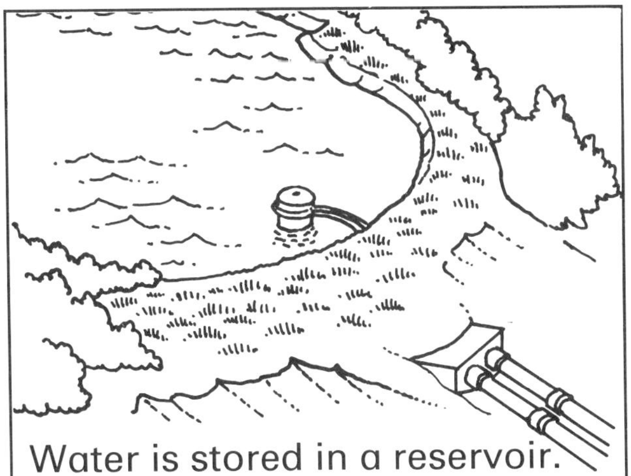

Water is stored in a reservoir.

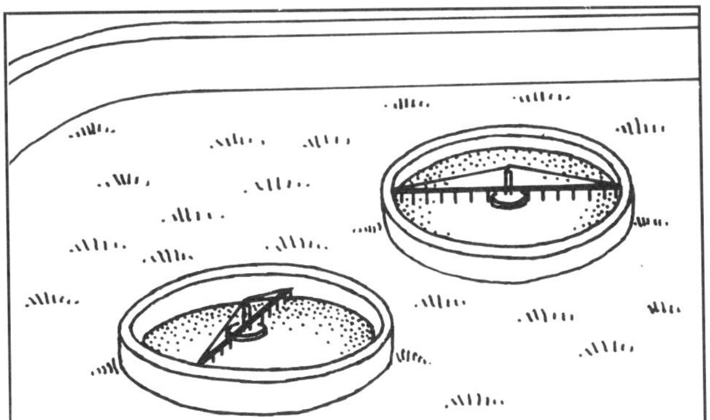

Waste water goes to the sewage works.

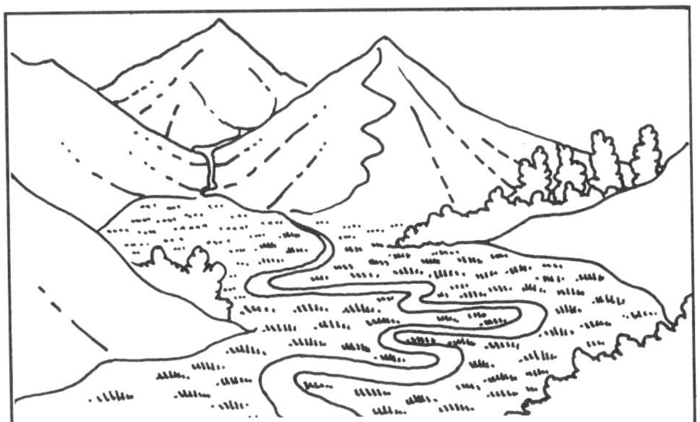

Water is collected from rivers and rocks.

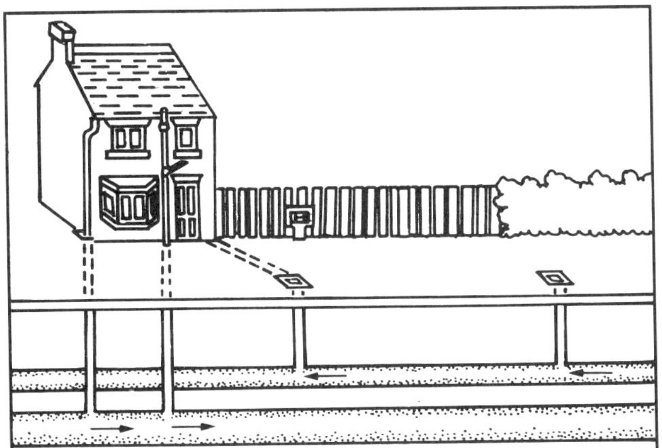

Pipes take water to our homes.

Rain falls in showers and storms.

Name ______________________________

Worth preserving?

1. Make a survey of the outside of your school building. Begin by naming three different views.

View 1 ______________________________

View 2 ______________________________

View 3 ______________________________

2. Now answer the questions in the table using the scoring system shown below.

yes (good)	3 points
average (OK)	2 points
no (poor)	1 point

3. Add up the totals.

Questions	**View 1**	**View 2**	**View 3**
Is it in good repair?			
Is it made from good quality building materials?			
Are there attractive decorations?			
Are the windows interesting to look at?			
Does the skyline make a good silhouette?			
Does it look welcoming and friendly?			
Does it have any historic value or importance?			
Total			

4. Which part of your school seems most worth preserving and why?

____

____

____

____

Name ______________________________

School improvements

1. Describe your ideas for four different school improvement projects on the file cards below.
2. Think about each one and colour the circles to show if the project involves new buildings, repairs or trees and plants.

Project 1

____
____
____
____
____
____

new buildings ○	repairs ○	trees and plants ○

Project 2

____
____
____
____
____
____

new buildings ○	repairs ○	trees and plants ○

Project 3

____
____
____
____
____
____

new buildings ○	repairs ○	trees and plants ○

Project 4

____
____
____
____
____
____

new buildings ○	repairs ○	trees and plants ○

Name ______________________________

Improvements trail

1. Draw arrows linking the labels to the correct part of the picture.

derelict land covered with weeds and rubbish	empty buildings with broken windows	trees snapped off by vandals	temporary car park

graffiti (writing on walls)	heavy lorry causing noise, fumes and vibrations	ugly advertisements

2. Make a list of problems affecting your area in the table below.

Problem	Street or place

3. Discuss how each problem could best be overcome.

Name ________________________________

Special sites

1. Devise signs or symbols in the spaces below.

nature reserve	ruins	historic town	beach

2. Working as a class, or in groups, make a list of local sites.

Nature reserves

Ruins

Historic towns

Beaches

Name ______________________________

Different landscapes

1. Look at the list of landscape features. Award points for the things listed in each column. Give 4 points to the feature you think most attractive, 3 points for the thing you like next, and so on, finally giving 1 point for the thing you like least.

Landscape features

shape of the land		**water**		**land use**		**buildings**	
mountains		streams		moors		ruins	
hills		rivers		forest		old houses	
lowland		canals		farms		church	
coast		lakes		parks		castle	

2. Working from photographs, draw two different landscapes in the spaces below.

3. Name each place and award the correct number of points for shape of the land (relief), water, land use and buildings.

Name of place		**Name of place**	
shape of the land		shape of the land	
water		water	
land use		land use	
buildings		buildings	
Total number of points		**Total number of points**	

4. Add up the totals to find out how the places compare.

Name ____________________

National Parks

1. Draw lines linking the labels to the correct places on the map.
2. Colour the different National Parks.
3. Which National Park is closest to your area? ____________

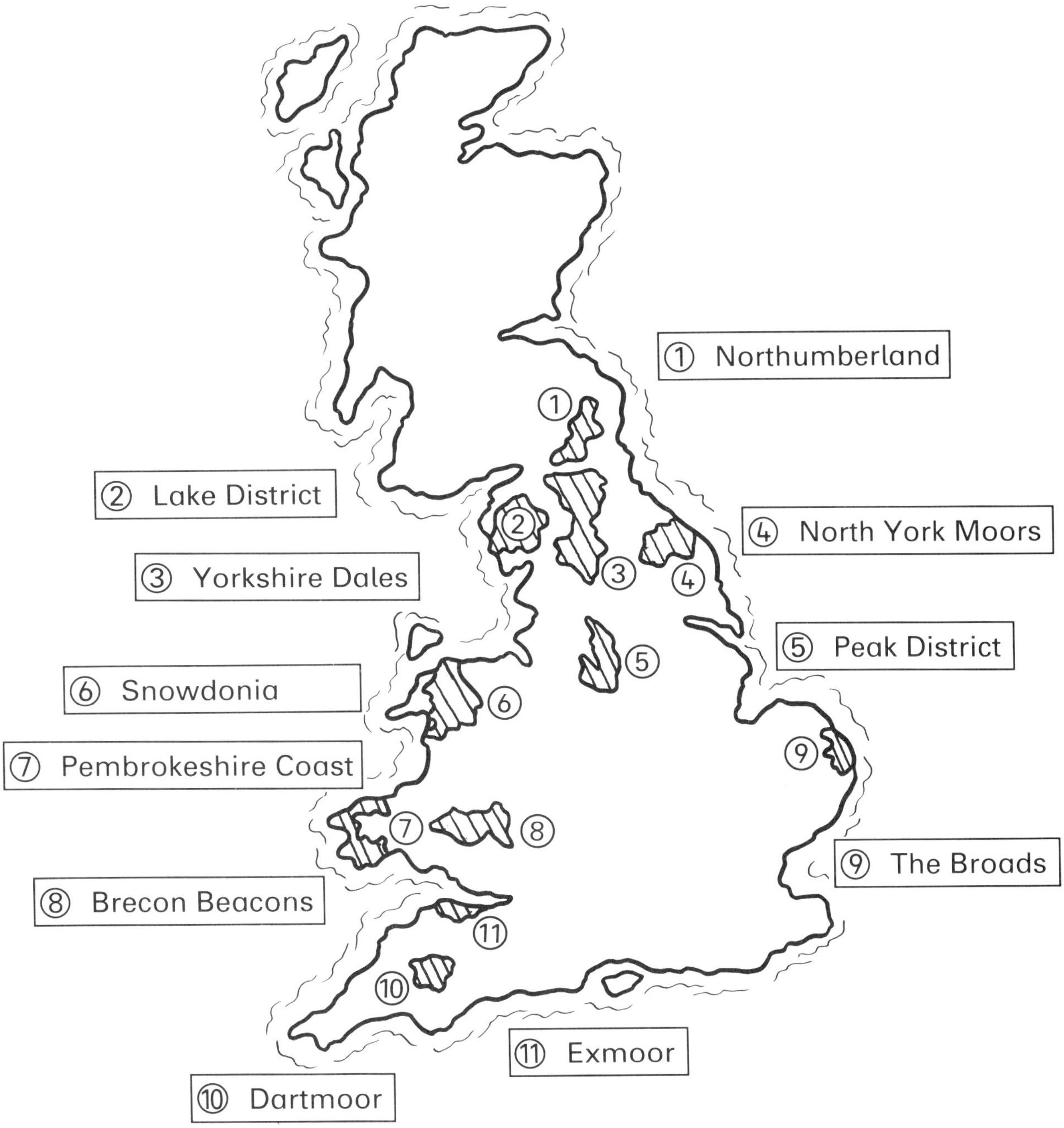

Geography KS2

Use ticks to show which copymasters pupils have completed.

	Title of copymaster														
Name of pupil															

PUPIL PROFILE **Geography KS2**

Name of pupil ....

Name of school ....

Record pupils' progress using these symbols
A: Above average S: Satisfactory
H: Needs help to make progress

Year	Projects studied	Achievement: Skills	Achievement: Places and themes
3			
	End of year summary		
4			
	End of year summary		
5			
	End of year summary		
6			
	End of year summary		

Pupils who consistently need help will be working at level 2 or 3.

Pupils who are consistently satisfactory or above average will be working at level 4 or 5.

Level at end of KS 2 (circle)

2 3 4 5